Nine M on the Outside

By

C. N. Mingo

Copyright © Cathy Mingo Nov 2023

All rights reserved, including the right to reproduce this book, or portions thereof in any form. No part of this text may be reproduced, transmitted, downloaded, decompiled, reverse engineered, or stored, in any form or introduced in any information storage and retrieval system, in any form or by any means, whether electronic or mechanical without the express written permission of the author.

ISBN: 978-1-3999-6986-4

Nine Months on the Outside

by

C. N. Mingo

God was my guiding light during these nine months, whenever I felt that I was unable to cope, my faith helped me through, praise and thanks to Jehovah.

I would like to dedicate this book to my wonderful son Wesley, who made it through the nine months and is now a 17-year-old.

I also give praise to my eldest son Jude, who was also a beacon of support during this time always believing that Wesley would come home no matter how many rollercoasters we had to ride.

Prelude

I was pregnant at 40. I'd always said I would not have a baby if I was over 40, but I was 4 months along, in my second trimester, when I visited the Commonwealth of Dominica for my cousin's wedding. I had her wedding dress and various other things. The wedding was the best I'd been to, but it was 2006, the year of the E. coli epidemic. In Dominica it was called the 'running sickness' because it caused vomiting and diarrhoea. Of course, we were not aware of that at the time, and I got it and so did my son Jude.

We flew home 5 weeks later. We'd had a good holiday, and I had rested and not travelled about much, but even so I went into labour on the plane. I started spotting, an ambulance was called and when we landed I was taken to East Sussex Hospital in Redhill. I was scanned and I was still bleeding, but they did not think I was going into labour, although he was lying low. They gave me steroids to mature his lungs.

It was a stressful time. I had to speak to the doctor on duty and convince her that my child would survive and that he was worth saving. She finally agreed that even though my baby was only 23 weeks and 1 day, if he came out crying and breathed on his own, he would be intubated and stabilised and moved to a hospital that could best cope with his needs.

I held onto him for two or three more days and then went into full labour. It was night-time and the shift had changed. All the plans that were in place had not been cascaded down to the nurses and midwives on duty. In fact, I had the midwife who had not been briefed; she did not know the plan, so she proceeded to stroke my arm and tell me it would be over soon. I screamed at her to call the people outside, shout my name, tell them I was in labour. I screamed at her through the pain and the gas and air of childbirth to get help, but she was reluctant. I remember saying to her, "I will close my legs until you call them outside." As soon as she did a stampede of people came into the delivery room, just in time for my little man to be born.

Honeymoon

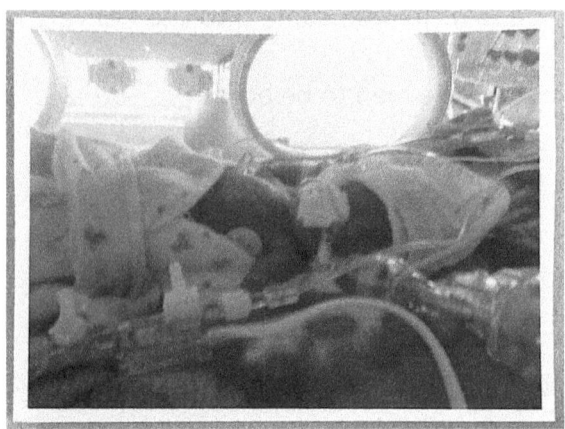

26 August 2006

Day 1 (23 + 3)

The time was 10:59 pm and I had just given birth to a baby at 23 weeks and 3 days. He was a boy. He weighed 540 g (1 lb 3 oz). I'd had a couple of days to think about names. I had called him Wesley.

The birth was just as painful as if I had given birth to a full-term baby. I had gas and air. I recall thinking that was a blessing at the time.

When Wesley was born, I remember lying on the bed with my eyes closed, willing him to take his own breaths and cry. It felt like I waited for hours, but it was only a few minutes. When he did take his own breaths, he was immediately put on life support. It took 5 hours to stabilise him. He did not need resuscitating; he was my little soldier from that point on. He was transparent and the colour of a strawberry, but he was gorgeous to me, and I loved him instantly.

I was not able to hold him because he was too small. He was also too young to be cared for at East Sussex Hospital; they did not have the right equipment. They arranged to have him transferred to St Peter's Hospital in Chertsey. He was critical but stable. Before they took him to the hospital in Chertsey, they took a picture and that is all I would have of him before I saw him again.

I remember not being able to control my racing heart. I felt like I was looking at something or someone else; this was not happening to me. All I had done was go on holiday. I had been so happy – I felt blessed, pregnant with my second child.

I had not known he was a boy, but I felt so good. I had not envisaged this.

Usually when you have your little one, they are handed to you, but for me that didn't happen. I had just given birth, but I had nothing. I had gone through the pain and the anguish, but my arms were empty.

I took one final look at Wes. He was stable and in a transportation incubator. I looked at my little man who could fit in my hand. His beating heart and his veins stood out through his transparent skin. It was a shock to see, but the love I felt for him was overwhelming. I just wanted to protect him.

The next day the midwife told me I had not delivered the full placenta. I needed a D&C, or to use the more common word, a scrape. My boy was so small. Why hadn't they got this right? Or rather, why hadn't I got this right? Somehow I felt this was my fault. And there would be more trauma before I could see my little man.

27 August 2006

Day 2 (23 + 4)

I woke, or did I? I was not sure if I had got any sleep. Distress is not the word – maybe 'shocked' sounds better. I had not slept very well. I remember thinking, *I couldn't even get the birth right. The placenta didn't want to leave my body, but my baby wanted to – he couldn't wait.* I recall thinking it was unfair and I felt like I was floating.

They put me on the maternity ward. Whose idea was it to put an already traumatised mother there? I was in a side room, but I had not lost my hearing, so I could hear mothers with their crying babies. I remember lying down and feeling empty, like something was missing.

When I got out of bed to call St Peter's, I had to leave my room and go onto the ward to use the phone at the nurses' station. There were mothers and new-born babies everywhere. In that moment I could not feel myself walking and I could not hear. I walked down a tunnel and everything was white. I know I made the phone call, and I was told my boy was critical but stable. He was very small; he could go downhill very quickly; he was so tiny. I don't remember returning to my room – it was such a blur. I had given birth and I had nothing to show for it.

The next thing I remember I was going into a very clinical-looking room where there was a doctor looking at an ultrasound and saying that not all my placenta had come away. They did the D&C and I was transferred later that day, thank God. The next memory I have is being in the ambulance and finally being taken to my boy. He was too far away from me. I could not think straight.

The NICU

I remember thinking, *He will have been taken to the NICU*, the Neonatal Intensive Care Unit. This opened a whole new world of neonatal care.

There were so many babies in the NICU. Some were ready to go home; their parents had been through weeks or even months of visiting the hospital and were now ready to leave. They had a special 'going home' area for parents to stay in, so they could look after their baby for a few nights, knowing that they could call on the professionals. They had gone through the process; they were ready to go home. All I remember thinking was, *Will I be able to make it?* It was going to take months – did I have the strength to do this? On top of everything else I was being told, I needed help to do this, but where was that going to come from? And what about Jude, my firstborn, who was 11 years old and just starting secondary school?

28 August 2006

Day 3 (23 + 5)

I was getting ready to see my son for the first time since his traumatic birth. I did not know how to feel. I was shaking, excited, anxious and very tearful. I wanted it to be happening to someone else. I could not do this; I was not strong enough. I remember asking God, *Why?*

Have you ever had the feeling that your feet are just so heavy you don't know how you put one in front of the other? It felt like my steps were so small and it was about a mile from the going-home room to the NICU, so no matter how fast I walked, it took longer than it should have! At one point I thought I had stopped walking.

When I stood in front of the doors, they opened automatically and I was immediately overwhelmed by the noise. There were beeps, bells and talking; there were lots of equipment and pods. At least, that's what they looked like to me: pods with wires going into them, numbers flashing on screens – so much flashing and noise. Where was Wesley in all that chaos?

He was near the window, which I thought was nice; the sun would be good for him. I saw my son for the first time since he had been taken away in an incubator. I was given two more pictures of him. I saw lots of lines going into the incubator, and among all the wires I saw a perfectly formed baby as big as my hand.

"He needs his respirator tube changed."

"He needs what changed?"

It was dangerous considering his size. They hoped to put the tube to his stomach down through his nose instead of his mouth, so he could be fed. Also, the hole between the two main blood vessels leaving his heart was not closing on its own, its official name is a PDA - Patent Ductus Arteriosus, which is present in a baby and will keep the blood flowing around the body from the placenta. Once a baby is born, this hole closes automatically, and the lungs take over with taking in oxygen and blood flow around the body. In Neonates, if born too early, this does not close automatically and medication or a small operation (where a clip is put on to close it permanently) is required.

Medication is given. If it does not close, the baby will retain water and so cannot have all the feeds that would help them to grow as they will blow up like a balloon. So, he was being given medication to close it. That medication could cause problems; we would have to wait and see what happened.

I felt very scared – he was so tiny. Was he my baby, this small little thing you could barely see inside that big pod of an incubator? I later found out the incubator was climate-controlled – the temperature could be turned up or down – and it was quieter than the room was. It was also not a good idea for light to stream in, so they always had a blanket over the top of the incubator to keep it as dark as possible.

I just watched him. He had a line in his hand for medication; he had a feeding tube and the life-support machine, which was helping him breathe. He was connected to a screen via tiny pads on his chest that were checking his oxygen levels and heart rate. If all was well, the machine was silent, but Wesley kept moving and it kept going off, which made me anxious, before I knew his movement was causing it. They kept checking on him and putting up his morphine, but it just seemed to make him worse. They said he was a fighter, and he was fighting to survive. As time went on they told me more about medication and the things I would have to do to help my son survive.

29 August 2006

Day 4 (23 + 6)

I blamed myself for so many things. For travelling to the West Indies. For allowing myself to listen to the doctors who said it would be fine to fly, that I was at a good stage in my pregnancy. For not leaving Dominica when the sickness really took hold. What if I had not gone at all? The scenarios I played over in my mind were endless, but in truth hindsight is a wonderful thing and can have you creating happy endings just based on what-ifs!

I woke up in the morning blaming myself, but I realised that Wesley was in the hands of God and I could not blame any one situation for what had happened to him. I just needed to hope and pray for his well-being. And that I would receive some support from Trevor, Wesley's dad, when he gets over himself.

30 August 2006

Day 5 (24)

As a Catholic, I had to get Wesley baptised tonight. I named him Wesley Mervin Prosper Mingo Richards. The priest said I would have to complete his baptism when he was out of hospital. (I realised when Wesley was 2 years old and had the water sacrament that he was given the last rites that night.)

Trevor was once again not happy. How could I talk to that man? He had so much blame in his heart. *Lord, give him time to realise that holding onto anger and blame will make him even sicker.* Trevor was sick, he had been since 1988.

Trevor did not believe Wesley should have been baptised. He said it "put pressure on the little guy". I think he was scared but would not admit it.

31 August 2006

Day 6 (24 + 1)

Wesley was still the same, no change. I was told in the night to expect a phone call during the day. "We're reducing his meals, but we're pleased with his progress." I got no explanation as to why I would be receiving such a phone call, but I later found out that Wesley was so small, he was in what they called the 'honeymoon period', and after a week things could change and he could get very sick and not survive.

I found the person looking after him upsetting. My feelings about her meant that, again, I had a bad night. She was not reassuring – she said if anything was going to happen, it might happen at night.

Wesley was having his tube changed this morning. *God, please guide the hands of the doctors, ensure they are fully guided by you. If Wesley is being cared for by non-believers, please be the guiding light for their hands.*

Wesley was now 1 week old. He had not grown; he was still very small. I did not want any pictures of him with his cuddly toys – they were bigger than he was. There was a lot I didn't know and didn't want to know at that stage. He had survived the week, and I was told that after this point it might all go downhill. I was praying and holding on to God.

September

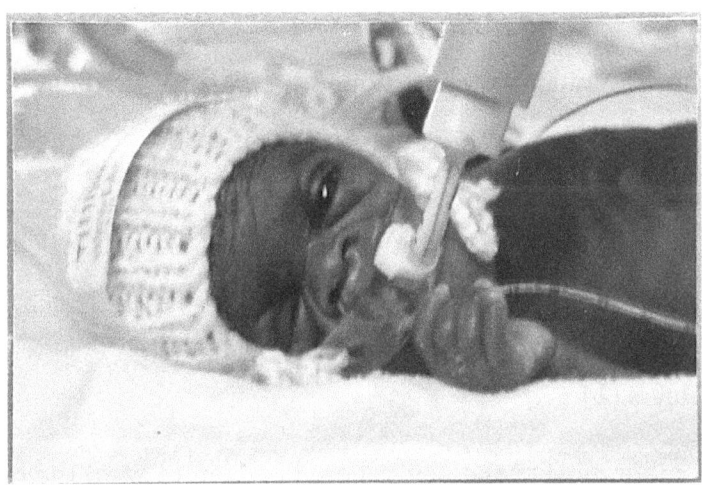

1 September 2006

Day 7 (24 + 2)

Wesley seemed very well in himself. He was very still and slept a lot, although by the evening he was wriggling and moving about. I spent the day at the hospital with Jude. He became very tired, bless him; he has had to grow up very quickly.

I looked at my 11-year-old son and wondered what he could possibly be thinking about all this. He was proud to be a big brother, but there was such a long road to travel, how would he be able to handle it? How would I handle it? He did not say much to me. I hoped he was not holding anything back, but how would I ever know?

2 September 2006

Day 8 (24 + 3)

I spent most of the day at home and left to go to the hospital at 4 pm. So began another tradition: Jude would stay with friends on a school night, while I spent the night at the hospital with his brother.

Baby Wesley had pulled out his tube and had to have it replaced. He also had the pressures put up. There was a lot of information that I needed to digest. The pressures were part of the life-support machine – they kept the air flowing at a steady rate to keep him alive. The gases were good, which was a good thing. If they were low, it meant he was not getting enough oxygen going round his body and there was hope that the hole outside his heart had closed.

It had been 8 days and I could not really remember what had already happened, except for when I made notes in my diary. I didn't want to retain any information. It was so overwhelming, I had to take one day at a time.

That was easier said than done, to be honest. I saw how small Wesley was and could not imagine him being any bigger. Was I lacking faith in God and the doctors and nurses who were looking after him? I felt helpless. I should be holding and feeding my baby, getting him into a routine, but now I found myself holding onto the words of the nurses and doctors who were keeping my boy alive. I remember thinking, *In the real world, this would not be happening. I would have control.* But for now, this was not my domain. My little man was in the hands of God and at the mercy of the health professionals.

3 September 2006

Day 9 (24 + 4)

Wesley had a crisis and I went to the hospital with a friend. They had a bed set up for me, but I did not need it – he stabilised. Wesley had a restful night.

His dad had still not admitted to being scared. Did that matter in the grand scheme of things? Trevor turned off his phone so he could not get any bad news. I remember thinking how lucky he was that he could turn his phone off and pretend there was nothing happening.

This was going to be a journey. I went to the hospital with people who prayed. I found comfort in having like-minded people around me; it could only be a positive thing for us. They really helped me to talk about Wesley and pray for his progress.

Jude was having to step up as a father to Wesley. I did not want that, but that is what I could see happening, and it was only because he wanted to support me.

4 September 2006

Day 10 (24 + 5)

I got to the hospital at 3:50 pm because road accidents had slowed up traffic. I spoke to Dr Thomas Owen. They were trying new meds to close the hole outside Wesley's heart – another 5-day course. Wesley had stabilised and there had been a reduction in his blood gas numbers. The ventilator had been reduced and he was comfortable for the night.

I was told that this new medication could disintegrate his bowel, but there was only a small chance of that. If they didn't use the medication, they would have to operate on my little sprat of a boy. He was still no bigger than my hand. I was sure he had not put on any weight.

5 September 2006

Day 11 (24 + 6)

Wesley was unstable; his oxygen was going up and down, caused by the hole that needed to close. This was the second of five days of medication. He was also on antibiotics.

I said prayers tonight, as I always have. This was Wesley's most unstable time, in Jesus' name.

6 September 2006

Day 12 (25)

Wesley was very unstable and needed 100% oxygen. He had been put on an oscillating ventilator. This came with its own risks – it could cause brain damage. Could I refuse the treatment because of that, and if I did and he went downhill, would it all be my fault?

His gases improved greatly and he only needed 25% oxygen this evening. I went to my friend's house for prayers and to give thanks.

7 September 2006

Day 13 (25 + 1)

Wesley now needed 40% oxygen since his ventilator had been

adjusted. Norma, one of the neonatal nurses, also said the consultant had raised his morphine to 20%, but he still kept moving. *Lord, guide the doctors today to reach the right balance with Wesley. He is in your hands, Lord.*

Wesley had a very stable day, in Jesus' name. I went home tonight because Jude needed his mummy. Another neonatal nurse, Bina, was looking after him.

The past few days with Wesley had been the most challenging. He was up and down; his oxygen was up and down. We were waiting for the hole to close, and much as I liked to think the medication would work, it had not so far. Wesley's oxygen level was a bit worrying; he'd needed 100%. The oscillating machine shook him – it looked awful, but I had to realise that he was very sick and some of these methods were experimental in one so young.

8 September 2006

Day 14 (25 + 2)

Wesley had a comfortable night. He had the line in his arm changed so they could give him medication, because the one through his belly button had fallen out. He was now more comfortable, thank you, Lord.

While all this was going on, life was continuing outside the hospital. Jude had got onto the school football team. Well done, number one son!

Tonight, Wesley was very stable. Nothing had changed – he was comfortable and his hole had begun to close, so hopefully that would help with his oxygen loss. His milk had been increased. I was going to see him the next day. I had not seen him today, but I was looking forward to seeing him tomorrow. Sometimes I stayed away because I could not cope with seeing my son so helpless, and I felt helpless having to trust people I had just met to be mother to my child.

There was one nurse at the hospital who kept going on about how she did not want to fry her ovaries, so she left the NICU whenever a little one needed an X-ray. If *she* was worried, what was the danger to my little man? I understood they needed to check him, but did that mean his insides were being fried every time as well? Little things and questions I did not want to ask, or answers I did not want to know. It had only been a few days and it felt like months. How could I do this?

9 September 2006

Day 15 (25 + 3)

I spent the whole day at the hospital; Jude did not come. Wesley's oxygen was a bit high, and he was stable when I left. I went round to my friend's house and we said prayers for Wesley. Jude went to football.

I didn't know what I was feeling or even how I was supposed to feel, but it felt like my insides were constantly shaking. I would have conversations and they would always make me feel like I was not doing enough. Should I smile? Could I feel happy? Or should I feel guilty for doing things other than looking after my sick little boy?

10 September 2006

Day 16 (25 + 4)

Jude went to football. I phoned the hospital and they told me Wesley was stable. I went to Elim Church in Watford and spoke to Pastor Guy Miller. I did not know it at the time, but he would become one of the cogs in this wheel that was turning so slowly. I took one of his cards; I would call for his help to pray for Wesley. I did not know then how important Pastor Guy would be to me and to my relationship with God on this journey.

I phoned the hospital again and then went in because they said Wesley was quite bad. When I got there, he had stabilised.

11 September 2006

Day 17 (25 + 5)

Wesley was back on conventional ventilation and had been stable most of the day. When I called at 7:15 am, he was on 31% oxygen and stable. They were changing shifts.

I went to visit Wesley with Pastor Guy from Elim Church. I went to Watford first and then he followed me to the hospital on his motorbike. That was cool, although he said that I drove very slowly, even in the fast lane – he did not know a black woman could drive so slowly.

Pastor Guy came up to see Wesley and we prayed over him. He used the Book of Psalms and my Bible. When we had finished, he asked me what I wanted, and I said to have my son healthy and at home.

He said, "We have prayed and taken your request to God, so I will tell you now to let it go. You have brought it to Him, you don't need to keep asking Him. Just let it go in the mighty name of Jesus. This is my final request. Watch over him, Lord. Cover him with the blood of Jesus. Watch over him, Lord. He is with me in prayer."

All I said was, "He is in your hands, Lord, you know what I desire."

Wesley's head scan was okay. He was stable. Jude was happy there was no more karate on Mondays, the day was changed, he was working towards his black belt, but he also wanted to play football, which was on Monday.

12 September 2006

Day 18 (25 + 6)

Wesley was stable. There had been no change, although he was retaining a lot of fluid. *Jesus, give the doctors the knowledge to help him, bless their hands.*

However, he was not being fed and it looked like he was developing an infection. He was on two types of antibiotics for different things. His oxygen was good, between 23 and 33%.

They did not tell me what was wrong with him, just that he had some kind of infection. I spoke to a consultant and he said if something happened to Wesley's bowel, there would be nothing more they could do.

I remember thinking he had come this far, surely I wouldn't have to say goodbye to him, but the reality of the situation was that he was only 18 days old. That is no time in the world of a neonate – no time at all.

I realised at this point that I was getting into a routine: check his pressures, check his oxygen, check his blood count for infections, check if the hole has closed, ask when he will be taken off the ventilator, check if the medication is affecting his bowel. He kept moving, so he was given more morphine, but that seemed to make him move even more.

13 September 2006

Day 19 (26)

I saw Wesley today. His stomach was distended and his legs

and genitals looked swollen. *What is ailing my son, Lord? Root it out. He is fighting it and he is still well in himself. I can't cuddle or hold him. Lord, make him better.*

I remember looking at Wesley and wondering if he was in pain. I wanted to take him home. I wanted to hold my boy and feed him and give him a bath, but that was not going to happen. I thought I would get to the hospital one day and they would say that he was ready to come home, that we'd got it wrong or there had been a miracle – but no. "He is very sick" was all I heard.

I registered Wesley as Wesley Malachi Mingo Richards, His dad said there were too many names, so we dropped the Mervin and Prosper (the names of my cousin I stayed with in Dominica), he was on my mind a lot during Wesley's stay in Hospital, he also called quite frequently from Dominica. Trevor attended the hospital today, he really seemed interested and he asked a lot of questions, but he wanted to know the worst-case scenario all the time. I just left it to God.

14 September 2006

Day 20 (26 + 1)

I felt weepy today, and I'd wept the day before. *Lord, strengthen my heart and hear a mother's cry for help.* I didn't visit Wesley because my throat was sore and I felt like I was getting a cold. I needed rest, but I still felt tired.

Wesley was stable all night and his tummy went down a bit; it seemed to be full of wind. *It's in your hands, Lord.*

This was a rollercoaster – one minute up, the next minute down. My mind was in turmoil. I had been told the first week was the honeymoon period and then he could fade very quickly, but we were on day 20 so surely that meant he would be fine? Why did I now have something else to think about? I felt like screaming. There were no guarantees. What was I doing?

15 September 2006

Day 21 (26 + 2)

Wesley was still stable – 'still stable', what was I expecting? The ventilator pressure was reduced, oxygen 30%. *Please, Lord, banish the devil inside him and make his tummy well. I know you can do it. My faith is with you.*

I went to my friend's house to pray, and I also called the prayer line at Elim Church and spoke with Pastor Guy. I told him I needed help.

I enjoyed praying in a group. We all asked for what we wanted the Lord to do for us. I remember Pastor Guy said to me that I should not be begging, just reinforcing. I felt like I needed help, but there was no one to talk with. I don't remember being offered anyone to talk with at the hospital. Maybe it was offered, but I felt so overwhelmed I might have dismissed the thought altogether. I felt at the time that if I spoke about it, it would somehow become more real.

16 September 2006

Day 22 (26 + 3)

Wesley was stable. His ventilator settings were slowly being reduced so he could breathe for himself with the help of a CPAP machine (a machine that gave him pressurised air through a mask). He had to try to breathe; he was breathing about 17% of the time and that kept rising. His tummy was smaller and an X-ray showed improvement.

Lord, he is in your hands. I know you will watch over him.

17 September 2006

Day 23 (26 + 4)

Wesley was very lively and stable today. His oxygen was good, and it looked like his tummy had gone down. He was on three types of antibiotics that would get rid of anything that was growing. His CRP (an indicator of infection) had gone down. I decided not to go in the next day as I had some bills to pay and money to sort out.

At 1:30 am I received a phone call. Wesley was very unstable; his stomach was disturbing him. My worst fear had always been that they would call me in the middle of the night and I would have to drive to Chertsey and I might not get to my little man on time and he would be gone alone. I decided to call Sally, a friend I met when Jude was at nursery with her daughter, we stayed friends for years, she was my rock through all of this, as was Pastor Guy and we had a conference prayer call. We prayed that we would get more favourable news.

I called the hospital back after 2 hours and Wesley was stable. There were two things we were looking for: that he did not need a massive increase of oxygen and that his belly did not become distended. I did not want to ask the question "Do you think he has a bowel problem?" I thought that would be tempting fate.

18 September 2006

Day 24 (26 + 5)

I spoke to Dr Owen at 3:30 am and he said Wesley had been stable for 50 minutes, but he might have a perforation in his bowel – the words I did not want to hear. He contacted St George's Hospital in Tooting, as they could perform any procedure that might be needed.

At 12 pm, on my way to St Peter's, I received a call. Wesley was being transferred to St George's, so I had to change my destination as I was driving on the motorway. I arrived in Tooting before him, at 2 pm. It was very different there. They were constantly on the go, working very hard, and they had a lot more rooms. I couldn't even remember how I had got there, just that I had spoken with my brother on the phone and he had given me directions until I got to Tooting. *What's a satnav?* It was like another world back then. I did not have a satnav and had never thought of getting one. Did they even exist? I don't remember at this point.

19 September 2006

Day 25 (26 + 6)

I remember feeling like I needed company all the time. I needed to speak to someone I knew, not a stranger. I needed to talk about what else was going on in the world, I needed a distraction, because once I entered the hospital there was no place for small talk. This was not a world that anyone else could know about; it felt like a dream.

I travelled to Tottenham by car from Luton with my friend Daniel this morning. The journey was longer, but I felt that I needed to do it. I got on the Underground to Tooting Bec, very tired, but it was good that I stayed overnight.

They found a hole in Wesley's bowel. He would eventually have to have an operation to cut out the part of his intestine that had died, to join up what was left. At that point they were talking about giving him a stoma as they felt that, because he was so small, anything else would prove unhelpful.

20 September 2006

Day 26 (27)

I had an 11-year-old – it was not something I could forget. Was it right that I was not with him as much? I felt guilty whenever I spoke about Jude or thought about how much he needed me. He began secondary school, and I was not there; I did not help him settle in.

I took Jude to the hospital to see Wesley as he was having a problem with his teachers because of his hair. He needed a haircut, but I was at the hospital, so I took him out of school. There was no need for useless phone calls from the school.

Wesley had been stable since being transferred to Tooting, and they were beginning to understand his moods with my help. Today I was told that he might not need surgery. "I just want my son to have the best care that will help him recover," I said.

Wesley had his tube changed; his mouth was

restricted by a special knitted preemie hat that held the tube in place. I was feeling guilty about Jude, but he told me he was happy, he had a brother, he was no longer an only child. All the while I kept thinking that it would be months before we could be a family at home, but I had to be strong, I had no choice. I had to protect and look after my boys.

21 September 2006

Day 27 (27 + 1)

Another day, another feeling. I drove to Leagrave station, then sat on a train from Leagrave to London and then on the Underground to Tooting, but I still couldn't work out how I got to my destination. I had made this journey several times over the past few days – which would turn into weeks – but I always thought, *Did I float here?*

It was fear of the unknown every time. I could hear my heart beating all the way there, and I felt like I stopped breathing whenever I entered the hospital, until I found out how Wesley was doing. I realised that the feeling I was having was anxiety.

I saw the surgeon. Wesley's X-ray showed a leak in his intestine, so the operation would go ahead at 6 pm. I was so strong in my imaginary world, but I was dying inside. I did not have time to digest what was happening because a little girl called Sarah stopped breathing on the NICU and had to be put on a ventilator. Two other mothers (one of whom was Sarah's mother) and I were all praying for each other's children, that they would survive.

We held on to each other and prayed – three mothers praying for this one child, knowing that tomorrow it could be any one of us.

22 September 2006

Day 28 (27 + 2)

All the time that my boy was in surgery, I just kept wondering, *how are they able to do this operation? He's so tiny, so small, how in the world are they going to find the problem? How?*

After 28 days Wesley had not really grown any bigger. Because of his bowel and heart problems, he could not be fed, he could not grow.

Wesley's operation went well. He now had his intestine on the outside to give it time to heal, and he had a bag attached to it for his stools. *Is he in pain?* I had a bed in the hospital and I sat up watching him, waiting for his bowel to start working and wondering if he was in pain. He was too sick for me to hold, too sick for me to cuddle. Because his pain threshold was quite high, he had lots of morphine, but they had to wean him down so his bowel could start working. When was that going to happen? How quickly? How would they know the right time?

Jesus, please watch over my boy. Help him to heal so he does not have so much pain.

He was stable tonight, which was a blessing, but it just seemed like they were not telling me everything. Paranoid and scared – the default setting for me and for all us parents/mothers of one so small and helpless. We never knew if the medication was experimental if it had worked before. No two children were the same and the treatment was always different. 28 days and I still felt like we were on an unstable bridge; as soon as they stabilised one support, another needed fixing.

23 September 2006

Day 29 (27 + 3)

Out of all the conversations I had with doctors, consultants and surgeons, only one thing stayed in my mind: Wesley needed to come off dopamine. He was being given it for his blood pressure, related to the surgery he'd just had. I had a conversation with the doctor after Wesley's operation and he said, "We have to ensure the bowel is working, but also that he can hold his own blood pressure – we will know when he comes off the dopamine." This stayed in my head; it was a big thing for me, I fixated on it, but it was part of the process and the recovery. Every day I kept asking if he was off it yet. I phoned again, but I was only told the good bits.

I knew he was sick, but I knew he would survive, that he was in God's hands. *Wait on the Lord – that is what I must do. Help Wesley, Lord. Make him better.*

I had a bit of a breakdown while I was speaking with the surgeon. I felt like my head was going to explode. His ventilator pressures had been reduced to 19 and his oxygen levels were being left alone, allowing Wesley to recover by himself, but what about the dopamine? It was amazing that out of everything that was being said, I held on to the blood pressure meds. The morphine had not been reduced, his bowel had not started working, he still could not be fed, but I only heard and wanted to know more about the dopamine.

24 September 2006

Day 30 (27 + 4)

I was so upset about the dopamine, because in all the conversations I was having, that was all I heard – he must come off it. When he was finally taken off it, I couldn't stop crying. The dopamine was gone – surely that meant he was going to be okay? But he just seemed so restless today.

We were going to Luton. Or rather that was the plan, but Luton kept running out of bed space. Wesley also needed the hole outside the heart closed and they were trying to arrange this, but it was proving difficult. We had got a room in Ronald McDonald House, which was in the grounds of the hospital at Tooting, we stayed there for the past few days.

I went to church and Pastor Guy allowed me to get all my feelings out. I felt that it was wrong to cry. I had to be strong. If I kept crying, I would not stop and I felt that I would not be able to cope or look after Jude.

25 September 2006

Day 31 (27 + 5)

Jude's bus did not show up this morning, so he came to the hospital and saw his little brother, which was nice. Wesley was off the dopamine and he had two more days of antibiotics to go. His stoma was working, and he would come off the morphine and take paracetamol, The morphine would stop his bowel from working, so they had to stop it for a while. His pressures were down to 18 and the number of breaths had increased to 60 per minute, as they wanted him off the ventilator asap.

    Also, he would be eating soon, my strong little boy. I had been expressing milk for the past few days, for when he was ready, but because he was born so early, my milk supply was very limited. I kept being told that the more I expressed, the more I would get, but it was not working for me. I drank fennel tea because this somehow stimulated the milk flow, and I was eating and drinking, but the hormone prolactin automatically allows you to produce breast milk once you have a baby. My levels did not get high enough, because I had him so early, it was not giving me enough milk for Wesley. I was failing again. This was something I could do to help my child and it was not working.

26 September 2006

Day 32 (27 + 6)

Wesley had a peaceful night and he looked well within himself. But how did they know? How did I know? The surgeons were not worried about his tummy; they said it was a muscular problem, Lord have mercy. He would start his feeds in a couple of days.

I decided to go home with Jude at 9 pm. Wesley had been very stable all day, lying on his stomach. Thank you, Jesus. I went home because I did not feel useful, I did not feel like I was able to help Wesley. I could not feed him; I just sat and watched him and gave him comfort by putting my hands over him (cup holding). Small babies like Wesley do not like to be touched; they open their arms and hands to tell you no, and then they desaturate (lose oxygen in their blood) very quickly. The saturation machine should read between 90% and 100%, but because Wesley kept moving, it kept beeping, so we just had to watch him to see how active he was and then we were able to manually judge his saturation.

27 September 2006

Day 33 (28)

Wesley was stable all day. He had been taken off his morphine and we were waiting for his gut to start working.

I did not go to the hospital today, as I needed to express milk and get my body back to producing it for my little cherub. I was using the breast pump and still only getting about 5 ml, but I got 10 ml earlier today. Such a small amount, but it was like survival liquid for one so small. I had to fight for every ounce, but I knew it was his best chance.

28 September 2006

Day 34 (28 + 1)

The world sometimes reminds you that you live in two worlds, and both are out of your control. I was at the hospital when I got a call from Jude's school. He was unwell, so my mum (his nana) had to go and pick him up. My car had to be serviced, so I dropped it at the mechanic's and I would pick it up later. I had to check on Jude; I think he was overwhelmed and just needed to spend time with us. It had been about a month since Wesley arrived and our world turned upside down.

    Wesley was stable. His stoma was working and would start feeding him again soon. The doctors thought they had fed him too quickly at the last hospital, which was part of the reason his bowel had perforated. The bowel is the last part of the baby to develop, and when one is born so early, it needs time to mature. There would be a meeting tomorrow to decide not only what had happened but also consider the way forward. I recall thinking, *what do I do with this information?*

Sue them for mistreatment of my son, make a complaint? Surely all I can be is thankful that they are working so hard to save him, even if they make mistakes or do things differently? I would find as time went on that all hospitals use their own methods – of which there are many – to save and look after one born so early.

Later that day I met up with my friend. We talked and prayed in a group, before I went home with Jude.

29 September 2006

Day 35 (28 + 2)

We made plans to stay at the hospital this evening, at Ronald McDonald House. It would mean we were near Wesley and I could pretend to be a hands-on mother who just left him in a separate room while I was sleeping. He slept so well I was not woken up in the night.

Jude stayed with me; he had the day off from school as he was not feeling very well. He had nearly passed out yesterday. We were not eating very well – I think our diet then was burgers, chicken and pizza. Chinese food was a favourite, anything that could be made quickly. Ronald McDonald House had cooking facilities, but I still could not stand to cook. We ate junk food for lunch and dinner whenever we spent time with Wesley. Jude read to him all the time and we went to bed late.

If Jude was not with me, I would get a sandwich and eat in the parents' room. That was our escape from the unit, but it was scary to leave because you never knew what you would come back to. Sometimes I would stay there and watch *Deal or No Deal*, a new game show that most of us mothers enjoyed, although we always talked about the guilt of leaving our children.

30 September 2006

Day 36 (28 + 3)

28 weeks and 3 days – usually 12 weeks before birth. This is

when you're supposed to be showing and getting the room ready and looking at furniture and glowing. It's when friends plan a baby shower.

This was not my reality. In my neonatal world I was anxious. In my neonatal world I was scared. In my neonatal world I questioned everything. In my neonatal world I couldn't say no. I had to agree and pray that the doctors and nurses were blessed to do the right thing for my little man.

We went to see Wesley before breakfast and he was well in himself. We went back to Ronald McDonald House and had some breakfast. Jude had leftover Chinese food from the night before – what a great mum I am! Wesley was being fed and he seemed to be coping with it very well. They'd started him on 1 ml in a syringe and now he was up to 5 ml; that would increase slowly to make sure he was okay with his feeds. I couldn't feed him because he could not handle being handled, and that was another thing I beat myself up about.

When we went home this evening, Wesley's pressures were down on the ventilator – good news. I felt very tired, very relieved.

October

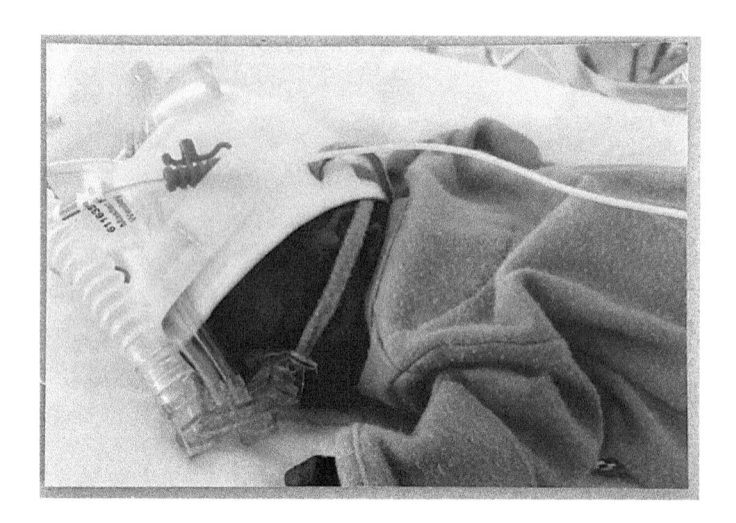

1 October 2006

Day 37 (28 + 4)

Jude went to footie with Daniel. He had a disappointing day – he only played for a minute. Why? Sometimes during footy they will bring a person on for 1 minute so they can at least have some play time. I questioned this as he was an established player and one of the best on the team, so why only 1 minute. I felt he did not get his chance to play because I was not there.

I went to church in Watford and really enjoyed it. I prayed for my boys.

This was the gospel song I had sung for inspiration.

Alleluia Alleluia!

For the Lord God Almighty reigns

Holy Holy

Are You Lord God Almighty.

Worthy is the Lamb

Worthy is the Lamb

You are Holy Holy.

Are you Lord God Almighty

Worthy is the Lamb.

Worthy is the Lamb

Amen

I went to Tasman's house to pick up Jude, new phone destroyed, I cannot recall what happened to the phone, but just remember thinking it was careless. Wesley was fine. I would visit him tomorrow night and stay at Ronald McDonald House.

2 October 2006

Day 38 (28 + 5)

My milk expression had gone down, and for it to pick up I needed to drink more and eat better food. I took all the milk to the hospital and it did not thaw out on the way, thank God.

The consultant told me that if the hole outside Wesley's heart did not close, they would have to go in and clip it. The operation would be done at Royal Brompton Hospital by special heart doctors. I was not looking forward to it. He was still very small; he'd had one major surgery already and we were talking about doing another one, again major, to do with his heart. *God will look after you, Wesley.*

3 October 2006

Day 39 (28 + 6)

I woke up very early. Wesley had a steady night and I went to see him at 9 am. I fasted until noon and I would do so every morning, I was fasting and praying, it is a powerful way to pray as you lay yourself bare to the lord when looking for answers. It is making a sacrifice.

Wesley's oxygen was up, his pressures were up and he was losing oxygen through the hole, the valve, the duct – I was to discover that there are many words to describe it, but its official name is patent ductus arteriosus (PDA).

When I left, Wesley was having an echo on his heart. I wondered what would happen. I phoned again when I got home and they said the hole was still there. The doctors would discuss it and let me know tomorrow. It was a waiting game.

My dad, Wesley's granddad, visited Wesley. He was going to emigrate to the West Indies in a couple of days. *God's hands are healing.*

4 October 2006

Day 40 (29)

I contacted the hospital this morning. Wesley had pulled out the tube of his mouth – his feeding tube, his lifeline, his only way to gain weight – and so he had no way to be fed. The nurses seemed to take it in their stride, but I felt like my heart was going to break. His oxygen changed from 30% to 40%; he was beginning to rely on it more, which was not a good sign.

Wesley was very active today and he kept setting off the monitors, but the noise had begun to feel normal to me. He had put on 10 g, which meant he was now 740 g (well done, sweet pea!). He had a restful day, no changes.

5 October 2006

Day 41 (29 + 1)

Wesley had a good night. He was stable and he put on 10 g,

so now he was 750 g. His gases were very good, so the ventilator could be adjusted by a small amount. He would have surgery at the Royal Brompton on Monday to clip the hole outside his heart.

6 October 2006

Day 42 (29 + 2)

I saw Wesley's dad this evening. He could not handle that Wesley had a stoma; he did not want to talk about it. His other son had had a bowel operation, so maybe it was hereditary, but he just did not want to talk about it.

7 October 2006

Day 43 (29 + 3)

Trevor sent a message – he would not be coming to the hospital today. I called him a coward by text message. He was not there when I was pregnant, so why should things change now? He's always doom and gloom.

One of the hardest things was going through this on my own, but I realised that if I was going to make it to the other side, the only people who mattered were Wesley, Jude and me and my faith in God. Nobody else was part of the picture unless they wanted to be there and look after themselves and work alongside us. I had my hands full with my boys and no space for another child, grown up or not.

8 October 2006

Day 44 (29 + 4)

I apologised to Trevor and left it at that. I had nothing more to say. Why did I apologise? What I'd said was true, I thought he was a coward, and as I type this I wish I had told him that.

Jude and I went to church. While we were there, I tried to engage with the service, but Wesley was on my mind all the time. I turned off my phone in the hope that there would not be any messages for me. What would have happened? I would have either a bad message or no message about

Wesley from hospital. I had received numerous, "please get here as quickly as you can" or 'things are not looking good right now'.

I heard my name and looked up at Pastor Guy. He was calling me up to the pulpit to tell my story about Wesley. I did not have time to prepare what I would say. I told them about my miracle boy who was born at 23 weeks and how, against the odds, he had cried and taken his own breaths. I don't think they could believe what was happening until the pastor explained how small Wesley was and how he had already had an operation. Pastor Guy had been shocked to see the size of Wesley; he was as big as his hand. I said he looked like a big rat; he was so thin you could barely see him.

After my story the congregation began praying. Wesley was having the operation on his heart in the morning and we all prayed for him, and that the hole would close and he wouldn't need the operation. *Bless all the hands that will touch him.*

9 October 2006

Day 45 (29 + 5)

Wesley was transferred to another hospital, the Royal Brompton near South Kensington, the most prestigious heart hospital in England. I remember arriving at the hospital and telling them that I was waiting for my son, who needed the hole outside his heart closed.

"He is in the best place for that," they told me.

It's funny, but that did not bring me comfort. I did not feel comfortable waiting for Wesley to arrive. When he did, the staff looked shocked that he was so small. They talked about the size of him, wondering how they were going to find the hole in one so small. They had never seen a baby so small. That just made me question why he was there.

Wesley was transferred for his operation. I was so happy that he would finally get the hole closed and he would be able to be fed properly so he could put on weight; Now I just wished they would send him back to Tooting and leave the duct. I was not feeling comfortable with my surroundings at this hospital. I felt the lack of care towards my son was very noticeable from not only the staff, but as I was to find out later, the consultant and his assistant.

The top consultant came to me and said that the hole had closed on its own. I was so happy, but when I questioned it, his assistant told me that he was the top consultant and asked why I was questioning him. I said, "We have waited so long for it to close, for it to have closed this morning is unbelievable." I felt like I was being told off.

Back to St George's we went. The consultants there were not convinced. They said they would check again tomorrow.

Did I believe the hole had closed? I think God did his work and the Royal Brompton was not the right place for Wesley to have his operation. It was the top heart hospital, but they seemed scared. Looking back, I think the consultant just didn't want to waste his time on one so small – he was choosing who he would operate on. What a git.

10 October 2006

Day 46 (29 + 6)

So, drum roll, the hole had not closed. It was there like a beacon, flashing away. In Tooting they did not even use the machine – all they had to do was increase his feeds and he blew up like a balloon. How had the top surgeon missed it? Because God closed his eyes to the miracle that is my son. I am convinced the surgeon did not think it was worth his time to operate on my boy.

There would be a meeting with the Royal Brompton on Thursday to find out where we could go from there. At that point I thought they could keep the Royal Brompton – I told them I would not be happy for Wesley to go back there. The top consultant said the hole had closed, and when I questioned it I was told, "You're questioning the top surgeon in the country. If he says it's closed, then it's closed." So much for being the top surgeon – he got it wrong.

The next few days were a waiting game. I prayed for a miracle and God gave me one, but not how I expected it. That hospital was not the right one, or the time was not right – either way we were still on the journey and I knew it was going to take time, but was I the right person for the job? Every day was a day closer to going home. I just had to believe, I had to wait on the Lord.

11 October 2006

Day 47 (30)

I did not go in today. Wesley had his food increased to 6 ml per hour and the diuretics had been stopped. I was so happy at this point that the hole had closed – I would not believe otherwise, even though we already knew it had not.

12 October 2006

Day 48 (30 + 1)

I went to the hospital. Wesley had put on so much weight that his tube holder had become too tight and needed to be loosened. Although he was waterlogged, he still wasn't given any diuretics. The hole had not closed.

13 October 2006

Day 49 (30 + 2)

I stayed at the hospital this evening to see Wesley in the morning. I spent all day there and went home late and picked Jude up from Tasman's house. Jude was going to football the next day; Daniel would take him and I would pick him up from Tasman's.

14 October 2006

Day 50 (30 + 3)

I expressed a good bit of milk. Wesley was well today.

So let us address the elephant in the room. I have not written any long entries about the hole and the fact that it had not closed. I have made no mention of the arrogance of the top surgeon and his stool pigeon, or their lies about the hole being closed. I was disappointed at being told one thing and knowing in my heart that it was a lie. I was praying for God to keep control of Wesley's life and I was also praying for a different hospital. My prayers were answered, but as I said, not in the way I expected them to be.

15 October 2006

Day 51 (30 + 4)

I did not visit today, but I phoned. I went to Elim Church and did not mention Wesley. Jude went to football. Wesley now weighed 790 g.

When you have a child early, you pray for them to be healthy, but with health comes weight, so at some point it becomes an obsession, especially if your child is eating and doing everything else well. At that point Wesley was still at St George's, and as I saw him gain weight, I became more convinced that the hole had not closed.

16 October 2006

Day 52 (30 + 5)

Wesley had put on a lot of weight: 40 g last night, so he now weighed 830 g. I was sure this weight gain was not good – he had not had any diuretics for a few days now, since 9 October. They were watching my boy suffer. It had to be stressing out his little body. He did not look like he had put on 'good weight'; he looked bloated and uncomfortable. I kept asking myself, *Is he my son? Am I his mum? I do not have any say in how he is looked after, I cannot argue with the nurses, but what if they don't do their best for him?*

As a parent you are thrown a bone every day: "Mammy, do you want to do his cares?" These are done hourly and consist of dipping a cotton wool ball in water to wet his lips, using a syringe to feed him through a tube, changing his nappy three times a day. He did not wear clothes; the incubator kept him warm.

I was upset with some of the nurses in the NICU. They treated us like children, like we were not very helpful. They were in charge, we just had to follow the rules.

17 October 2006

Day 53 (30 + 6)

I did not visit Wesley today. Last night he put on 60 g, so he now weighed 890 g. His weight gain bothered me, but the doctors did not seem to be worried.

The echo showed that he had a moderate-sized hole that needed surgery. *It is your will, Lord*. I had a very strange afternoon after I heard this. I was scared. I could not watch Wesley puffing up like a balloon and feel happy. Much as I wanted him to put on weight, I could not deal with what was happening with him right now. I hated all the medications, but I felt like screaming "Give him the furosemide!" because that would get rid of the water he was retaining.

18 October 2006

Day 54 (31)

Wesley had his tube changed early this morning. He was not weighed, and he was desaturating a lot. It turned out the tube was not in properly, and the pressures and ventilator settings went up because of the tube. I hoped they were reduced now. He was being fed every 2 hours, 10 ml less food as he was retaining water.

The Royal Brompton was full – it was God's work, I am sure – so they found us a place at St Thomas' and Guys (Tommy's) in Westminster. Thank God they had no space at the Royal Brompton – that place was scary. They were supposed to be the best heart hospital in the country, but they did not have a clue about Wesley and I did not feel comfortable around them.

19 October 2006

Day 55 (31 + 1)

Tommy's would take Wesley on Tuesday and the op would be on Wednesday. This still needed to be confirmed.

I did not go into the hospital today. I stayed home and expressed milk. Wesley now weighed 945 g.

We were about to travel, to start a new chapter at yet another hospital. I stayed at home. I wanted to prepare and ensure that he would have what he needed at the new hospital, wherever that might be. One thing you learn when you must keep moving around: nothing is set in stone. There is always a child who is sicker than your child and you get bumped, so although I had a date, it was all in God's time.

20 October 2006

Day 56 (31 + 2)

Jude and I stayed at Ronald McDonald House for the weekend. Wesley had lost all the water that he'd put on to show the hole was still open, it was a tactic used, alongside the scans taken of his heart. He now weighed 915 g.

I'll explain a bit more about Ronald McDonald House. When you buy a McDonalds at a drive-through, there is a collection place that asks for donations for these houses. There are also collection cups. The houses are a home from home. There are bedrooms with ensuite or shared bathrooms, a shared front room and a shared kitchen. There is a small garden. When it all got too much for us, we had a room in the house where we were able to come and sleep, and if I wanted to check on Wesley in the night, it was just across the car park.

Parents and siblings could stay, so Jude would stay with me and we would go into town to shop or eat or just relax. I always felt like I had a stone in my stomach that would get heavier the longer I stayed away from the hospital, and a pump in my chest that would increase the pressure until we got back and saw that he was still hanging on in there. *God, please help us.*

We saw Wesley before we went to bed in Ronald McDonald House.

21 October 2006

Day 57 (31 + 3)

I woke up early to express milk. Wesley had his eyes open this morning. When I spoke to him, he responded. I stayed with him until 10 pm; he looked smaller again. He now weighed 910 g.

Trevor visited Wesley at last, after 5 whole weeks. Sarcasm was my friend. Trevor spoke to Bella, one of the nurses taking care of Wesley. I stayed with Wesley till very late as I was feeding him. When I say it like that it almost sounds like I was feeding him with a bottle, or even breastfeeding, but that was not the case – I used a syringe. As time went by I would come to realise how important this was in the neonatal journey of my young son.

22 October 2006

Day 58 (31 + 4)

As I was expressing milk, I spilt my tea all over myself, but I left it and continued to express until I had finished. I was desperate to express milk – how else could I feel useful? I could not hold Wesley, cradle him or bring him home to his cot, and I was also failing in the milk department. He was born so early, my milk-producing hormone had not kicked in and I was not producing enough. He needed it to ward off infection and to live, but I could not express enough for him; it had to be mixed with formula. When I saw Wesley, I just wanted to hold him close to me, but I felt like I was getting a cold. He knew me and his eyes moved to find me. I sang to him, read to him.

I came home with Jude tonight. Wesley now weighed 860 g. I did not realise how important his weight gain was going to be for his long journey in the NICU.

23 October 2006

Day 59 (31 + 5)

I was ecstatic. I expressed 60 ml of milk for the first time – it was the highlight of my day.

Wesley was doing fine. Carol was watching him, but I was not happy. Carol gave us smiles and said she understood, but I was privy to a conversation she had about one of the other parents, who she called a flake. She could not understand why she was so worried about her child. She said she should give it a rest – some of these kids were going to die anyway. There was more and it was very unpleasant.

I phoned the hospital to speak with the consultant. Wesley now weighed 885 g. He would go to Tommy's on Wednesday morning for the op in the afternoon, stay on

Wednesday night and then be transferred to Luton and Dunstable Hospital, nearer home, on Thursday, where they had a bed for him. This was such a big move for him and the longest he would have travelled since he was born. He would be moved in an ambulance, in an incubator, with nurses and doctors, but I could not be there; I had to travel by train with Jude.

24 October 2006

Day 60 (31 + 6)

Today was the day before the operation, I felt very nervous about everything. I contacted the hospital – Wesley had had a good night, slept well. He looked well and enjoyed having his mouth cleaned. He had a sucking motion; he wanted to be fed.

Lord, Wesley needs to come off the ventilator. I know this is a journey, Lord, and he is in your hands. There was so much going on in my head, I didn't know which came first and which came last: ventilator, feeding, pressures, oxygen, saturations. If I had to think about them all the time, I felt I would lose my mind, so I only thought about something when it happened or when it was mentioned. It was the only way I could cope.

We were going to Tommy's at 8 am, staying at Ronald McDonald House tonight. Wesley now weighed 945 g.

25 October 2006

Day 61 (32)

Operation day. I was feeling very good about it. Wesley had not been fed since 3 am. Then I was told that his operation had been cancelled: 27-week-old twins had just been delivered at Tommy's and they now had no beds available. *Lord, he is in your hands.*

When I was told his operation had been cancelled, I was so disappointed, but again I held on to my faith. When the time was right Wesley would have the operation. It was still hard as we thought he would have this operation and then go to a hospital nearer to home – we were on a journey to get home, but first we needed a hospital home that we could stay in until we could go home for real.

Wesley had a good day. We held him for the first time and I was so proud to take a picture of my boys. My friend came to visit and she took a picture of me with Jude and Wesley.

I fed Wesley every time today and emptied his stoma bag; it took a long time. His op was changed to Thursday. As I said before, I did not keep anything in my head; I would wait and see what happened.

He now weighed 950 g.

26 October 2006

Day 62 (32 + 1)

Rescheduled operation day. I arrived at Tommy's at the same time as Wesley, after spending the night at Ronald

McDonald House with Jude and Tracy (the parent of a little girl called Angela who was born at 28 weeks and was doing very well; out of all the children we knew, she would be the first one to go home).

We travelled on the train. We had two suitcases and it seemed to take forever to get to Westminster. Once again I had this feeling in my chest. I felt sick knowing that I had to go to another hospital and explain what had happened and what was happening now. *Why?*

We did not really speak. I was just anxious to get from Tooting to Westminster. Wesley could not tolerate a change in pressures, so although he did not have a bad travelling experience, they found that the pressures on the ventilator had to stay quite high.

The nurses on the neonatal unit made me feel very relaxed. They brought Wesley in and explained what was going to happen with the operation and when he would be transferred to Luton. I went with him to the operating area and they explained that they were going to put a clip outside his heart to close the hole there. I prayed for my son and felt like I was floating. I felt someone's hand on my shoulder and they said, "It's okay, he's going to be fine." When I opened my eyes there was no one there, but in that moment my hair stood on end and I felt all warm and happy inside; it was a feeling I still cannot explain to this day. Wesley had the op successfully, and they did an echo to check the ligation was complete.

I spent the night at St Thomas' Hospital. If I had been there for anything else, I might have enjoyed the lovely view of Big Ben and Parliament.

He now weighed 980 g.

27 October 2006

Day 63 (32 + 2)

Finally, Wesley was going to be in a hospital closer to home, so I could go and see him with Jude every day. What a blessing that was going to be.

I contacted Luton and Dunstable Hospital to find out what the procedure was. There would be a bed waiting for Wesley from 1 pm, staff were available and transportation was booked. It was a scary time – Wesley was still upset by the operation he had just had, and he kept moving and protesting. Even at such a small size, this little boy was stubborn. He needed to be to survive this.

Everything went well. Wesley was transported to Luton, but he protested so much that he had to be heavily sedated with morphine.

He had been moved and transported twice in as many days, but now he was in isolation, in a bed with a heat ray. He had a good night, although he had a high temperature, so he was on 20 ml of morphine. He was not fed.

He now weighed 1.3 kg.

28 October 2006

Day 64 (32 + 3)

It was so good to be able to go and visit with Wesley and stay for a while, and to know that home was not far away. I could also be with Jude in some way. I was able to get a new sense of normal.

Wesley had a good day; I visited with him twice today. His pressures and Beats Per Minute (BPM) were reduced to 20 and 45 respectively. His oxygen requirements were going down, partly due to the hole being closed, and that meant that we could really start to feed him so he could put on some weight.

The doctors took some blood as he might need a transfusion and they needed to crossmatch. I did all his cares and checked his stoma; it was fine. He was slowly being fed. His weight was now 1.4 kg. They had to keep checking the oxygen in the blood, and to do this they needed to prick his heel and bleed him. Because he was so small, the blood taken from him left his body requiring more, which is why he might need a transfusion.

29 October 2006

Day 65 (32 + 4)

I went to mass today to give thanks for Wesley's transfer. I went to see him this morning and he had some desaturated episodes. His feed was up to 6 ml per hour. Glucose was stopped and morphine reduced to 10 ml. Oxygen was high, gases were okay. His tube was changed, and he had better gases and oxygen requirements. Pressures to 19 and heart rate to 40 bpm, he might need a blood transfusion, he might need iron tablets. They were aiming to wean him off the ventilator onto CPAP. It would happen, it would work.

30 October 2006

Day 66 (32 + 5)

Wesley had another tube change – there was leakage around

the tube, so he needed a bigger one. They wanted to put him on CPAP tomorrow. *Please, Lord, be with him, be with us.*

Trevor visited Wesley and me; he seemed to be more positive. He still said he did not believe in God, but I don't know. I went to prayers, then back to the hospital to see Wesley. He was fine so I came home.

He now weighed 995 g – he had lost 10 g. The weight change was upsetting, but I was told that all the scales weigh differently. The children need to be weighed every night, and although they always try to use the same scales, sometimes they must use what they can get. Suddenly weight became very important; it showed progress.

31 October 2006

Day 67 (32 + 6)

Wesley had always had a problem with morphine – the more he had, the more he moved, but because he was on the ventilator, they said he must have it as he was in pain.

When the morphine stopped, his pressures reduced; his gases were fine. He was put on CPAP as he was tolerating the ventilator with fewer breaths. He stayed on CPAP for about 9 hours but was then put back on the ventilator. For his first time off the ventilator, he did very well, but he was becoming very tired. He weighed 995 g, or should I say he *still* weighed 995 g.

I was upset, when Wesley got to Luton hospital, they were trying to take him off the ventilator, he was able to go on CPAP; when he got tired, they said they would have to put him back on the ventilator. They took him off the CPAP and the nurse sedated him before the doctor was ready and he flatlined, he stopped breathing because he needed help to breathe. The doctor then had to rush over and intubate him to put him back on the ventilator (life support). When I told them I was not happy with what had happened, it was like I did not exist. They said everything was fine now. What do you do when you have a preemie and you do not feel that he is being cared for properly?

"Nothing," one nurse said to me. "They are doing what they can to keep him alive. Anything else is just not important now."

I couldn't believe that she said that to me, but what could I do? I just wanted to rip her eyes out, but then they would ban me from the hospital and I would not be able to see my son.

November

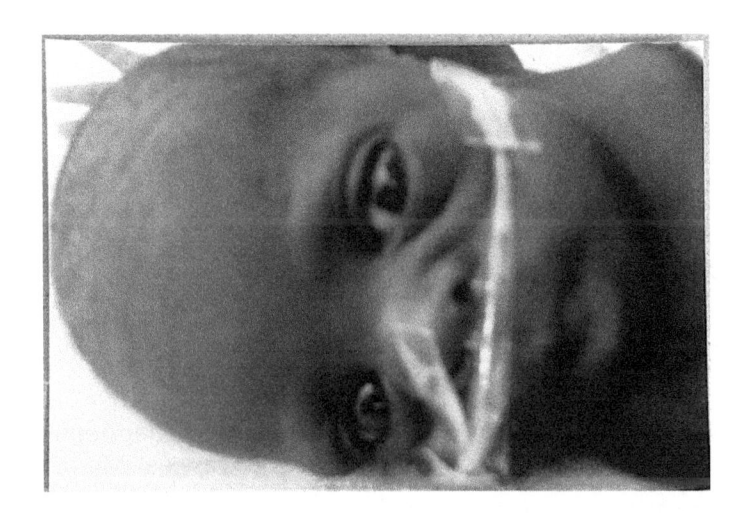

1 November 2006

Day 68 (33)

Pressures lowered to 22, with 40 bpm. Wesley was taking his own breaths about 50% of the time. Very active, not on morphine, back on full feeds of 7.2 ml per hour. He slept most of the day, so this evening he was wide awake. No sleep this evening.

It was lovely – I could now see him in the morning and the evening, which meant I could be there for Jude more. He was in his first year of secondary school and I had not been able to check or help him with his homework.

Wesley now weighed 1.02 kg.

2 November 2006

Day 69 (33 + 1)

Wesley was losing weight. What was happening? The diuretics would not help his weight gain either. What was happening? Ventilator pressures of 18 and 40 bpm. The aim was to wean him off the ventilator in the next few days. Next time it would be successful, by God's grace.

Wesley had an eye scan. Preemies are always at risk of going blind because the retina pushes on the eyeball. The optometrist checked all the babies regularly and Wesley was always being checked. The scan showed that he was at level 2, which was still good. At level 3 and above he would need laser eye surgery.

He now weighed 966 g – he had lost 54 g.

3 November 2006

Day 70 (33 + 2)

What was the new topic of the month? Oh yes, Wesley was now on CPAP all the time, and he was losing weight because he was taking breaths himself.

Today was eventful. I went in to see Wesley in the morning and his pressures were 18 and his heart rate was 30 bpm. They were giving him caffeine to keep him awake on CPAP. He went onto CPAP at 12:30 pm and at 12:15 am he was still on it, 12 hours later. His blood gases were good.

Imagine you are awake, but you don't have to do your own breathing because a machine is doing it for you. That's what it had been like for Wesley for the past few months, mainly because the hole outside his heart needed to close, but also because his lungs needed time to grow. Wesley was mad, but this was tough love – we needed him to be off the ventilator. He was losing weight because of all the changes and because he was using more energy breathing by himself.

They kept looking at everything, including his tummy, which was very big. Full of air, no doubt.

He now weighed 950 g.

4 November 2006

Day 71 (33 + 3)

Wesley was stable, tolerating his feeds and on BiPAP. BiPAP is an alternative to CPAP – it holds the lungs open, so Wesley did not have to work so hard to breathe. He was tolerating it well.

I bought Wesley some Babygro sets, mittens and socks. His clothes were so tiny, it was amazing. His stoma bag could be quite annoying: sometimes it was clean and stayed well, you wouldn't even know it was there; other times he had to have it changed twice because it began to leak. Still, he seemed well within himself.

He was starting to get used to BiPAP and all his gases are good, but he was losing sodium and they wanted to start him on a more fattening formula. I had a taste of the milk; it was salty, but he was being fed by tube, so he did not have to taste it.

He now weighed 945 g – still losing weight.

5 November 2006

Day 72 (33 + 4)

I was still going to church. I had several churches praying for Wesley, and it was so humbling. But I must say, the church in Watford with Pastor Guy and his family was the best.

Once I finished at church, we travelled home and then to see Wesley. Wesley had a good day. He was still on BiPAP, but his weight loss was bothering me. I felt anxious about it, but then I felt anxious about everything now.

Jude helped to change Wesley's nappy, we did Wesley's cares and emptied his stoma bag; his stools were more formed now, thank God. I took some pictures of him on BiPAP with the digital camera.

He now weighed 920 g, which was a further loss of 25 g. Who knew it takes so many calories to breathe?

6 November 2006

Day 73 (33 + 5)

Wesley had another good day today. He had started to suck his thumb and had been using a dummy for a little while. For the first time since having his ventilator removed, he cried and we heard him. He was getting his voice at last.

When we were in St Peter's Hospital, the nursing team gave me a book of psalms. They would use it to pray over Wesley when I was not able to visit or stay with him. I read this book to Wesley and sang to him while I held him. I joined a church in Luton and on Monday nights we had a sister's prayer group, we talked about sex, which was very random. We talked about maybe abstaining, about why we had sex, about having fun with it – although somehow I doubt it would be much fun thinking about the people in the prayer meeting, ha ha!

Wesley now weighed 975 g. His weight was going up again. That was the best news of the day, even though it was not even a lot of weight.

7 November 2006

Day 74 (33 + 6)

I woke up this morning and had quiet prayer time about faith. I was feeling a bit despondent, but it made me feel lifted. Jude was unwell.

I visited Wesley and got a parking ticket. I parked in a funny place, right by the bins, which I had to move slightly, but no one else would park there and I was desperate. If my car got scratched or damaged, I didn't care, if the engine was fine and it could get me where I wanted to be. So now I had to contest the ticket. I remember thinking at the time, *Life is still going on. No one knows – they see me coming and going from the hospital and nobody knows.*

Wesley was doing fine. His stoma bag was big, but it did not seem too big. Now he was only being given 10 breaths per minute and he was handling it well. Soon he would be on CPAP. He weighed 950 g – he had lost 25 g. Again, he was breathing more because they'd changed the settings on the BiPAP machine.

8 November 2006

Day 75 (34)

Wesley was doing fine. I did not visit much today as I felt that I might be getting a cold. He was put on CPAP. No breaths – he was doing it on his own now. This was when all his weight was going to fall off. How would he handle it?

I went to see him. He was doing well on CPAP, sleeping mostly. His kidneys and liver look fine, but he was being treated for jaundice. How could he have jaundice on top of everything else? That's what the big babies had, that's why they were in the NICU. How had he now got jaundice?

Sleep well, Wesley. Enjoy your new clothes. I'd had to search high and low, but they had a special set in Mothercare, so he was now wearing clothes.

He now weighed 965 g – it was going up steadily. *Until tomorrow.*

9 November 2006

Day 76 (34 + 1)

Wesley was doing fine. I visited only once today because I had a cold coming on and our ceiling was being replastered, thank God. I took in his Babygro's – he needed some more; he only had two.

He had another eye examination, which showed an improvement from 2 to 1, Preemies would generally go blind because the retina would push on their eyeballs. The eye specialist explained that the eye condition would be checked frequently over the next few weeks. Wesley never got to level 3 which would have meant laser eye surgery. Wesley went from a level 2 to level 1 which meant he was out of the danger zone and although his eyes were checked, it was not done as frequently. His next eye exam would be in a couple of weeks. His oxygen was between 40% and 43%. His feed had been increased to 7.8 ml × 24 (187 ml). He now weighed 1.03 kg – a rise of 65 g. After 76 days, he had not even doubled his weight.

Sleep well, Wesley.

10 November 2006

Day 77 (34 + 2)

I did not see Wesley today because I felt tired and rundown, like I was getting the flu. I thought I was just overtired.

Wesley pulled out his feeding tube and had to be put on antibiotics, just to make sure there was nothing on his lungs. If I had gone in, I would have seen what he was doing.

He had an X-ray of his lungs to check for fluid. He now weighed 1.09 kg – a rise of 60 g. His weight had gone up, but what a useless mother I was. The one day I could have made a difference and felt like a mum to my sick son and I was sick. He could have drowned from the inside because the tube was not in the right place and his milk machine was still running.

11 November 2006

Day 78 (34 + 3)

I visited with Wesley very early this morning. The antibiotics had kicked in already, but he was not very well – his oxygen was high and he was getting sick. Thank God the lady from last night was not watching him again.

My poor boy had to go through so much. His lungs appeared to be waterlogged. He was on the CPAP machine properly, no more life support. Although his oxygen had got up to 50%, it had now gone down to 35%. Well done, Wesley, love you.

He now weighed 1.08 g – he had lost 10 g.

I met Albert today.

12 November 2006

Day 79 (34 + 4)

Wesley looked well within himself. He looked bigger, although not too big – not holding water, I hoped. After I did his cares, he settled down quite nicely. He was very sleepy and although he opened his eyes to see me, he was not able to maintain it and he went back to sleep.

Building work was slow, Joseph the builder was slow.

Well done, Wesley, come on sweetpea. He now weighed 1.1 kg, a gain of 2 g.

13 November 2006

Day 80 (34 + 5)

Wesley looked good. His stoma bag had not been changed for a while, but today it was. I requested to see the stoma nurse and she said she would come on Wednesday.

Wesley was doing fine. He needed a lot of oxygen, but he'd put on a lot of weight today and he did not look fat. Trevor came, Trevor went. I held Wesley. He now weighed 1.75 kg, a gain of 75 g.

14 November 2006

Day 81 (34 + 6)

Wesley was doing fine. I held him this afternoon and he was upset when I placed him back in the incubator. I wanted to hold him more as it would hopefully stimulate my milk. I also had to see the doctor about domperidone, which helps to stimulate milk. He now weighed 1.19 kg.. Day 81, he had finally doubled in weight.

15 November 2006

Day 82 (35)

Wesley came off CPAP for 30 minutes, but his oxygen was too

high. He struggled and his oxygen was 75% of a litre. He slept a lot for the rest of the day after being taken off.

I saw the stoma nurse today, who went through all his stoma care and changed his bag. He would not have survived without the stoma operation.

He now weighed 1.21 kg, a gain of 2 g.

16 November 2006

Day 83 (35 + 1)

Wesley had a good night, but he kept desaturating. When I went in he was crying sporadically. It seemed to happen when his oxygen went high. He was in pain and all I could do was watch him. Was it the oxygen? Was he feeling unwell?

"What is happening, sweetpea?" *Lord, whatever is ailing Wesley, please remove it.*

His weight went down due to the weighing scales – really! Lord bless Wesley. He now weighed 1.15 kg, a loss of 6g.

17 November 2006

Day 84 (35 + 2)

Wesley had a good day. His oxygen went down and he seemed more relaxed in himself. The weighing scales they used were not consistent – maybe that would change; they needed to keep using the same weighing methods.

I held Wesley today. He was relaxed. He was not taken off CPAP. He now weighed 1.22 kg, a gain of 7 g.

18 November 2006

Day 85 (35 + 3)

Wesley had a good day. His oxygen level went down, and when I held him his oxygen was good. Jude was with me; he was also going to hold Wesley, but he started desaturating.

Another couple came in. They had their baby at midnight on Friday. She was very small.

Wesley now weighed 1.22 kg, no gain.

19 November 2006

Day 86 (35 + 4)

I went to see Wesley alone today. Jude stayed home alone! I held Wesley for about an hour and a half, longer than I had held him before. He was getting better; I could feel it. He was very relaxed, but wasn't he always relaxed? Maybe he was just not able to move around like he wanted to, but something was different when I held him. 'Bonding' – there's a word. When I had my first son, Jude, I did not think about that at all, but with Wesley I was thinking things like, *I am finally bonding with my son.*

    I did his cares. The rush I felt from this, I wondered if it was normal. I would look around the NICU and see all the parents doing the same thing – there was joy. I looked at my boy and had a rush of emotion. The Holy Ghost was in the NICU, that was how I explained it.

    Today I noticed people, I noticed other parents. Some had just arrived, were just starting their journey; others were getting ready to move to the High Dependency Unit (HDU), the next step to get ready for home. We were nowhere near going home.

Wesley had his eyes open. Because he had a stoma, I had never had to deal with a dirty nappy, not yet, but I did have to empty his bag. I was still learning how to do this without making a mess of the bag. There must be a way, otherwise how do people live discreetly? The doctor said he would try him again off CPAP to see how he coped.

I prayed with Wesley tonight and a couple of nurses joined me. *When two or more are gathered in Your name, You move among us.* It was a spiritual moment. I felt overwhelmed. I think I experienced what I thought was the Holy Ghost.

Wesley now weighed 1.155 kg, loss of 5 g.

20 November 2006

Day 87 (35 + 5)

Wesley was taken off CPAP. OMG, we could see his face! He had a face without a machine hanging off it! His nose looked sore. We took several photos, then Wesley's heart rate went very high due to a temperature. He was prone to infections and there were the endless blood transfusions. They had to take blood so often to check his gases that it did not have time to replenish, which meant blood transfusions.

Wesley desaturated quite badly so he had to be bagged. I was shaking when I heard this – isn't that what happened when they couldn't take their own breaths? What had happened to cause this? I went back in and did his cares; he was so alert. Were they sure this was the child they had had to bag? I asked them and they said, "He has had his blood transfusion."

Because he did not really sleep, he had his eyes open all night. He looked gorgeous, my sweetpea. His stoma bag was changed because it was leaking again. The umbilicus looked full of pus, so they took a swab and said we would get the results next week. I asked why he still had the umbilicus – that was normally gone by now, but he still had his, they were using it to feed him when he was at St. Peter's hospital. It should have dried out, but it just kept getting wet and I felt he was being neglected. Why had it not dried out? It normally did within 7 days of being born. Was Wesley being neglected?

You may not get the feeling that I was pacing and feeling very stressed, but my heart was racing and I did not feel calm. There was so much going on that I felt like I was on a treadmill that kept speeding up and then slowing down – a workout I had not planned but that I had no choice but to get on with. I never found out why he was bagged. He was so happy when I went in, it did not seem important.

He now weighed 1.17 kg (2 lb 9 oz), a gain.

21 November 2006

Day 88 (35 + 6)

Wesley had a good day. I visited with him and he was off CPAP. He was given oxygen manually, without a cannula, and he did well. I held the oxygen as he had a nosebleed and could not go back onto the pressure of CPAP. I decided I might not go back tomorrow as I was not feeling well; I seemed to be getting another cold.

We were not sure at this stage if he had had a nosebleed, they were now not sure, but I did know that he could not have the cannula in his nose. Again, when you have a child so small, can you complain about the treatment, or do you just have to be grateful that they are keeping your child alive with medication and machines and over-pumping them full of milk, so they put on weight? They are like calves being fatted for a special occasion. When the kids throw up, they just mop it up and continue.

He now weighed 1.18 kg, a gain of 10 g. He had gained weight again – only a small amount, but enough to make me have hope.

22 November 2006

Day 89 (36)

I did not visit Wesley. His feeds had gone up as his weight gain was very slow. He was not taken off CPAP today, but he did love his dummy. I had spoken to the hospital during the day, but I was not able to contact them at night because I fell asleep. He desaturated and his breathing became shallow, so they stopped his feeds and gave him antibiotics because he might have an infection. On the day I could not visit him, everything happened to him. I felt inadequate as a mum because my son was born early and suffering, and now he had gotten sick and needed antibiotics and I had not been available to sit with him. I felt even more guilty on top of the birth guilt. On that day I once again let my son down.

I stayed home and did not see my little miracle for one day. I phoned the hospital and tried to get some rest. For one day I stayed home and made dinner for Jude and myself. For one day I could do all my washing and drying. For one day I could wash Wesley's tiny clothes and pretend everything was fine. For one day!

He now weighed 1.21 kg (2 lb 11 oz), a gain of 3 g. He had put on a bit more weight than last night, but was it enough?

23 November 2006

Day 90 (36 + 1)

I found out what happened yesterday evening. I went into the hospital early to check on Wesley. He was asleep with his dummy, stable, with green bile coming out of his belly. His arm was swollen from the drip. *God will provide. I will not believe he has necrotising enterocolitis again.* Wesley was going to be home for Christmas by God's grace.

So, you are asking, *why was his arm swollen? Why the bile?* Well, if he had been born at full term and did not have to be kept alive and well with medication, I would have complained, but I just had to understand. The cannula in his arm failed, and so instead of going into his veins, it went into his arm, so his arm was full of water and we had to wait for it to be absorbed. His arm looked like that of a fully developed, full-term baby compared to the rest of him, which was small and scrawny. He had an infection in his umbilicus. They cleaned it up and it was fine.

He now weighed 1.27 kg, a gain of 6 g.

24 November 2006

Day 91 (36 + 2)

He was back on half feeds in the morning and full feeds by the afternoon. His stoma was working again. *Thank you, God.* This journey had been maintained by the grace of God.

Wesley's arm was still swollen. He did not come off CPAP today. Everything was so important, but I felt like my stomach was in knots all the time. *When this feeling goes, when he is all better and home and this feeling goes, where will I be? How will I feel?*

He now weighed 1.35 kg, a gain of 8 g.

25 November 2006

Day 92 (36 + 3)

Wesley was given a blood transfusion again because his haemoglobin (iron level) was low. He had been started on vancomycin (very strong antibiotics) because his infection markers were very high, so now he was on two antibiotics. His arm was no longer swollen. The second antibiotic brought down his markers from 40 to 11. Thank you, Lord.

So much had happened over the past few days, what with Wesley getting sick and his arm getting swollen, that sometimes I just had to sit down and think, *how long, Lord, how long? I am walking with only one set of footprints and I know it is because you are carrying me. How much does my little man feel? How much will he remember? Does he feel pain?*

There was so much with Total Parenteral Nutrition (TPN) and milk and antibiotics and everything else. They took blood from his heel to check his markers, but they took too much and he needed a blood transfusion. So much!

At 3 am he was well and settled. He now weighed 1.365 kg, a gain of 15 g.

26 November 2006

Day 93 (36 + 4)

Wesley had a good day. He was still on his antibiotics, doing well. The doctors decided to try him off CPAP and he did very well; he went over the hour. He was on 75% oxygen and they said he would probably be taken off again this evening – we would see.

The doctors said Wesley might have a condition they needed to check. If Trevor, the sperm donor, and I gave blood, then they would not have to take what little blood Wesley had to test it. Guess what? Trev refused. I do not use bad language, but if I did I think the pages would turn blue – forget the writing. So, they took Wesley's blood for testing, which would take about 12 weeks. I was always on my own.

He now weighed 1.33 kg, a loss of 35 g.

27 November 2006

Day 94 (36 + 5)

Wesley lost some weight today – only 5 g, but he needed to put on weight. *No more losing weight, sweetpea.*

Wesley's aspirate was stricken with blood from a previous nosebleed. Everything else seemed fine – he came off CPAP for an hour and Jude held him. I loved seeing Jude hold his brother. They bonded so well, my heart felt like it would explode. Wesley's saturations were so good when he was being held by Jude.

Wesley now weighed 1.325 kg, a loss of 5 g. At some point I would have to realise that his weight was not something anyone had control over. There was so much to learn about a child who was on the NICU. They are so sick, but to deflect from this the staff give you things to grab onto, things to look forward to. Weight is just one of them, their feeds are another, blood gases and nappy changes, how much water and poo have they passed.

28 November 2006

Day 95 (36 + 6)

Wesley was doing well. They were keeping an eye on his tummy, but he was off all his antibiotics. Today he came off CPAP for over an hour.

They changed his stoma bag; it was wet with urine. Jo, one of the nurses looking after Wesley, was going to leave him wet with urine on his stomach. It was so hard not to knock her block off for leaving him in that state. He had just been on antibiotics and keeping him with a urine-soaked stoma bag on his stomach would surely cause him some problems – sore skin, blistering. But if I created a fuss, would that mean my son would not be looked after properly? I kept my mouth shut and my heart joined my stomach in knots. I felt like I was internally hyperventilating because I could not let Jude or anyone else see how upset I was.

Wesley now weighed 1.31 kg, a loss of 15 g.

29 November 2006

Day 96 (37)

I visited with Wesley very early today. He was fine; he was asleep and wearing the CPAP mask. I did not wake him up.

The facial mask was causing his nose to bleed. He came off CPAP for an hour again and he enjoyed it. It took him a while to settle. The dietician saw Wesley and said that she would take up his case, because of his poor weight gain, she was asked to do this by his doctors. His stoma bag leaked and was changed.

He now weighed 1.355 kg, a gain of 45 g.

30 November 2006

Day 97 (37 + 1)

Wesley had a good night, back on the CPAP. The doctors decided that he should come off CPAP twice a day, morning and evening. He was taken off at 12:30 pm and then again at 6 pm. He was now breathing very fast and his food had been stopped so he could have an X-ray. It might damage his lungs, so this was stressful – this whole entry is stressful!

Wesley's feeding tube was not in properly, so his milk feed went onto his lungs. They had to stop his feed and ensure the milk came off his lungs; if they had not caught it in time, he could have drowned from the inside. OMG, I could not speak out, I could not knock anyone out. I had to hold it all in while feeling like I was going to explode. *The devil is a liar, God is in control.*

He now weighed 1.28 kg, a loss of 7 g.

December

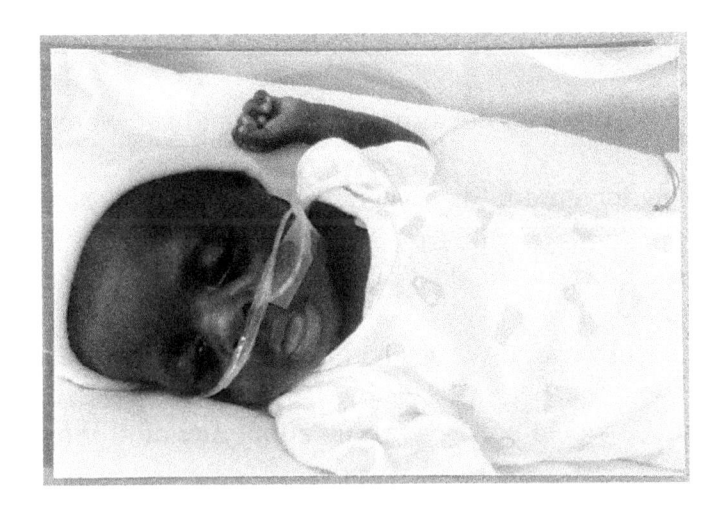

1 December 2006

Day 98 (37 + 2)

Wesley had recovered and was now stable. It might seem like what happened was nothing, but it could have killed him if something else didn't. His lungs would have filled with milk and then he would have just gone. Who was supposed to check it? Whoever it was, I don't think they did, but any complaint I made would not actually mean or do anything. He was a very sick boy, still weighing under 5 lb, and sometimes

I felt like I didn't have a leg to stand on where Wesley was concerned.

Wesley's needs had started again and were gradually being increased. His oxygen was between 35% and 38%. All this jargon – what did it mean? Why did I need to know this? The truth was, if Wesley had not been born early and on the NICU, I would not have a clue about any of it. Why would I need to know this? I was not a doctor or a nurse, I was his mum.

I was angry about Wesley being taken off CPAP twice in 5 hours, but again the staff were not paying attention, not writing down what they are doing so that at changeover they could see what had happened. It would be so easy for Wesley to have another crisis and end up back on life support.

I would do Wesley's cares tomorrow morning if they had not been done. Hopefully he would come off CPAP tomorrow, and his stoma reversal had been pencilled in for 8 January. I was not sure how I felt about that – he was alive and there were more important things to be doing, so surely that could wait?

He now weighed 1.28 kg, the same.

2 December 2006

Day 99 (37 + 3)

Wesley was very stable overnight, back to full feeds and the glucose drip had been stopped, thank you, Lord. Wow! It was such a relief that, although there was no real improvement, Wesley was back where he was before he became dehydrated and got an infection. This whole episode felt like I had gone further down the hole and the light was so dim I could barely see it. Now we were back to halfway and I could see the light shining brightly.

Wesley had a stable day. His oxygen requirement was quite low, 31%. I spoke to the doctor about taking Wesley off the CPAP machine and they said 1 hour twice a day, once with me there.

He now weighed 1.35 kg, a gain of 70 g.

3 December 2006

Day 100 (37 + 4)

So began another day. Wesley was off CPAP for 40 minutes this morning at 6:30 am and he did well. Every time something happened, it felt like I had to press the reset button and we would start all over again.

He was nearly at the day that would have been his birthday if he had not been born so early; this was when they had said he should be ready to go home, but he was nowhere near ready. Wesley had had such a journey through different hospitals and not one of them did the same thing, but all the different methods had worked.

The doctors agreed again to do 1 hour twice a day; he was taken off at 2:25 pm - 3:40 pm. I visited with him and he did well. He was not struggling or gasping for air, so he would come off again later today, sometime in the evening, 11 pm perhaps. He did very well. Of course, he had lost some weight because he had to breathe for himself again, but I would speak to the doctors about it just in case there was another reason.

He now weighed 1.325 kg, a loss of 25 g.

He received his 100-day certificate. That was an achievement, but I so wished it was a certificate to say goodbye because he was well enough to go home. I was really looking forward to having him home for Christmas. This would also have been the birth date of his sister; she would have been 13 years old. RIP, little one.

4 December 2006

Day 101 (37 + 5)

Wesley was taken off CPAP for two and a half hours when I went in this morning. Well done, my little man! He did really well and he would be taken off again at 10 pm.

I had to talk to the doctors about his weight gain and loss. I was not sure of his oxygen levels, but he had lost more weight, again due to the time off CPAP – the more he had to breathe on his own, the more energy he used up. He now weighed 1.3 kg, a loss of 25 g.

5 December 2006

Day 102 (37 + 6)

Wesley was stable all day, 30–33% oxygen. He came off CPAP for 2 hours – he spent an hour and a half on me, in a kangaroo hug. I wore my cardigan and nothing underneath it, and I put Wesley inside my cardigan and buttoned it up. Skin-to-skin contact is such a healing thing for one born so early. I put him to my breast and he enjoyed the milk. I then made him suckle my breast and he was fine. Wow, breastfeeding Wesley! Such a big thing when he had been so unwell, but it was such a normal thing for me. I so wanted to breastfeed him.

He went back into the incubator and then came off CPAP for 3 hours tonight. Well done, Wesley. Thank you, Jesus. He was getting used to coming off again.

He now weighed 1.371 kg, a gain of 71 g.

6 December 2006

Day 103 (38)

Wesley was doing well – a bit wriggly, but they'd managed to wean his oxygen down to 30%. He was off CPAP for 3 hours and 15 minutes today. He was still on several medications, but he was doing a lot more crying now and needed to be held more. Again, he came off CPAP for 3 hours last night – well done, Wesley, praise the Lord.

He now weighed 1.39 kg, a gain of 19 g.

7 December 2006

Day 104 (38 + 1)

Now we just kept trying him off CPAP. He did well and we

waited. He had been crying more and he needed to get off CPAP so he could be held more. Today the doctors decided to try him off CPAP for 4 hours and he did well, 10% oxygen. Thank you, Jesus.

He had to have his bag changed twice today because it was leaking and there was a hole in it. He came off CPAP for 4 hours, on 20% oxygen from the cannula. Well done, Wesley! He also had a vaccination against chicken pox, praise the Lord.

He now weighed 1.431 kg, a gain of 41g.

8 December 2006

Day 104 (38 + 2)

Because he did well yesterday (6 hours off last night), Wesley was taken off CPAP for 6 hours today and he tolerated it very well. Pastor Guy visited him; he had visited Wesley in all the hospitals he'd been in, to pray with me and give me the strength to carry on. I held Wesley and Sandy, the nurse who was looking after him, put him to my breast.

"You did really well, Wesley."

He was coming off CPAP for longer and his weight was going up slowly. He now weighed 1.435 kg, a gain of 4 g.

9 December 2006

Day 105 (38 + 3)

Wesley had a very good night off CPAP for 6 hours; he tolerated it well. His feed was up, but I was not producing enough milk. I felt anxious, but Wesley looked fine; he looked so big now. He would come off CPAP again today, but I just couldn't help but be anxious about it. We always got so far and then he would get an infection and go back on CPAP again.

He was well and had the date set for his stoma reversal. We would be going to Addenbrooke's Hospital on 6 January and the operation would be on 8 January. I felt so anxious.

He was off CPAP for 8 hours today and tolerated it very well, so he would come off for 8 hours again tonight. 20 – 30% oxygen levels, yes, his oxygen levels were going up, and that is when I got even more anxious. *Thank you, Jesus, for holding him in your hand, and Lord thank you for covering him with the blood of Jesus.*

He now weighed 1.415 kg, a loss of 20 g. Do you see the pattern? The more he came off CPAP, the more calories he used. But then his oxygen started to go up and I said, "Not again, God, not again."

10 December 2006

Day 106 (38 + 4)

I held my breath when I went to see him. I felt sick, I was shaking inside, but Wesley was doing fine. They said that he did not seem to tolerate 8 hours off, but they would see. I felt like I was on a merry-go-round because we started off slow and it got faster, but instead of getting slower and stopping, we were chugging along and waiting – always waiting. The merry-go-round would change direction and it would feel like we were going the wrong way. All the signs pointed the wrong way and it was scary. While we waited, I changed his stoma bag.

Wesley was off for 9 hours today and tolerated it very well. They said they would see about increasing it later and what his tolerance would be. Nine hours last night. *So proud of you, little one. You are making us so proud. Thank you, Lord.*

He now weighed 1.455 kg, a gain of 40 g.

11 December 2006

Day 107 (38 + 5)

Wesley. I am always saying prayers for you, always praying before I come in to see you. You are my baby, but I am so removed from you. Do I have the right to ask for you to be cared for in a certain way? No, I must wait for them to tell me how they will care for you. I have no choice.

Wesley tolerated another 9 hours off the CPAP last night/this morning. Well done, sweetpea! He was taken off for another 8 hours today, and he tolerated it well. Thank you, Lord.

At prayer meeting, I did not mention Wesley as a special case. I remembered what Pastor Guy had said: "Leave it to God. You have told him what you want and now you must wait for him to do his work." It was so humbling to know that he was being prayed for by so many people, and he was surrounded by so many people who wanted to pray for him. *Wesley is being prayed for and is in your hands, Lord.*

Wesley's weight was a worry, but it would improve by God's grace. He now weighed 1.444 kg, a loss of 11g.

Depending on who I asked, they said the scales had changed or the weight was different because of the scales, but I really thought his weight was a problem and they should be doing more.

12 December 2006

Day 108 (38 + 6)

Just because I had not said anything about how I felt didn't mean I didn't feel it. From the time I left home in the car I felt anxious, like I couldn't breathe properly. I could feel my heartbeat and sometimes I couldn't even remember how to get to the hospital. When I did, it was a scramble to look for a parking space, so I did not have to pay for parking. I learned to squeeze my car in by the big bins and not care whether it got damaged on the outside, just so long as I could go in and see my boy.

Wesley was doing well. He was still being taken off CPAP for 8 hours a day and tolerating it well and tolerating his food. The doctors saw him and called in the dietician to assess his weight gain and loss. I held him for 2 hours; he was so relaxed.

It was open evening at Jude's new school. He had hardly anything in his books, there was so much going on. The teachers had good things to say about him, but his work had begun to suffer.

We did not visit Wesley that evening. I had to spend time with Jude; he needed me to take some time for him. Wesley now weighed 1.454 kg, a gain of 10 g. It was not enough.

13 December 2006

Day 109 (39)

Wesley tolerated coming off CPAP for 9 hours this morning by accident. They forgot he was off it and he was doing so well no one noticed.

The dietician was called to have a look at Wesley, but because he had necrotising enterocolitis, they were reluctant to give him more calories in the form of a powder. They'd increased his feed to 12.1 ml per hour, which he had tolerated so far. He lost weight today – because they changed the weighing scales, I was told. He now weighed 1.303 kg.

Did I believe what they were saying about the scales? No, I didn't, and they had no answers. In my head they were discussing things with us that they could make us attach to keep us away from the real issues: the infections, the saturations (or should I say desaturations), the swollen tummy and genitals. One minute you go home and everything is fine, the next you come back and your child is having a blood transfusion. Why? Because they keep taking blood to check the oxygen levels in their blood, and because they are so small it does not replenish quickly so they need more blood and platelets. It's all fun and games, or is it?

14 December 2006

Day 110 (39 + 1)

Wesley was doing fine, feeding well and he could be taken off CPAP for 10 hours now – well done, sweetheart. He had an eye test and the eye doctor said the next time he saw Wesley would be as an outpatient when he left hospital. The doctor was surprised that his eyes were so good for a 23-week premature baby. Eyes are usually the thing that goes in a child that has been born so early, but he surprised everyone.

He got sick twice and his feed was reduced. They overfeed them to make them put on weight, like turkeys at Christmas. Why do we think this is a good idea? Do we, or is it that we don't have a choice? Our babies would not survive without it and we just go along with it because *we don't have a choice*.

Back on CPAP early. God bless Wesley. Trevor visited today, looking like a scared rabbit. He kept looking around and said, "Look at all the men here. You can tell they do not want to be here." He was just looking for an excuse.

Wesley had gained weight so now he weighed 1.32 kg, a gain of 17 g. new weighing scales. Seriously? Probably not.

15 December 2006

Day 111 (39 + 2)

Wesley went on CPAP again at 9 am. I felt sick to the pit of my stomach. I wanted him off that thing; it had caused his nose to split. Today he did 10 hours off. Well done, Wesley. Thank you, Jesus.

I wanted to hold Wesley so much I ached, but I knew he needed this time to concentrate on his breathing. I prayed for him and with him, and thanked God for him.

I spoke to Trevor today and got upset. He just did not take any interest, not really. He hid his visitor's pass and behaved like Wesley did not exist. What can I write about him? He always came across like an honourable man, but he was in denial – he left me to deal with all of it. God help him and me. Thank you, Lord.

Wesley now weighed 1.56 kg, a gain of 240 g! The scales again? They did not have an explanation. I said new scales, old scales, fish scales. Nothing said about the scales.

16 December 2006

Day 112 (39 + 3)

Jude's birthday. Wesley was doing well. He tolerated 10 hours off again and was on the cannula again from 3 am – well done, sweetpea.

He had not gained 240 g; it was the scales again.

Wesley began to feel unwell. His oxygen requirement off CPAP was 75% and 60% on CPAP. He seemed to have an infection, so they were keeping an eye on him.

We went to watch Barnet play for Jude's birthday.

I'm not sure what happened with Wesley's weight today. He now weighed 1.303 kg – the scales again. What could we do about that? Nothing, we just had to listen and nod.

17 December 2006

Day 113 (39 + 4)

They took various swabs because they thought Wesley might have caught an infection from me when I was doing his cares and they discovered his stoma bag was leaking and needed changing. It fell off when I went to change it. All his skin was irritated; the bag was a disgrace. A swab was taken of the area, bloods were taken, an X-ray of his lungs, stomach – all fine. They started him on antibiotics.

I met Trevor outside. He came back to our house but did not visit Wesley today because he was caught in traffic. Wesley was not taken off CPAP because of his high oxygen requirement. He just wanted to cry and he wasn't moving a lot.

He now weighed 1.37 kg, a gain of 67 g.

18 December 2006

Day 114 (39 + 5)

Wesley didn't have an infection in his throat or nose, but we were waiting for the blood test results. His oxygen was still high.

Trevor came with us when we visited Wesley this evening. It was nice to see us as a family. Wesley should start to show some improvement soon. His oxygen was down to 55%, by the grace of God.

He now weighed 1.439 kg, a gain of 69 g.

19 December 2006

Day 115 (39 + 6)

They increased the phosphate for bone growth; the infection was finally subsiding. His oxygen was 35–40% throughout the morning. Well done, Wesley. *Thank you, Lord. Thank you, Jesus. Through you all things are possible.*

Wesley was back moving around as usual, setting the monitors alight, making them bleep. I hoped they would start taking him off CPAP again tomorrow, but his bloods were not back yet.

He now weighed 1.456 kg, a gain of 17 g.

20 December 2006

Day 116 (40)

Wesley was doing well. They'd stopped antibiotics and he was now more alert, his oxygen between 30% - 35%. He was dribbling a lot and needed to start bottle-feeding/breastfeeding – I would talk with the staff tomorrow.

He now weighed 1.479 kg, a gain of 23 g.

21 December 2006

Day 117 (40 + 1)

Wesley was stable overnight, taken off CPAP for an hour and a half. They put his feed up to 11.1 ml. He had a very sore nose from the CPAP; I would have to keep an eye on it.

I held Wesley for an hour while he was off CPAP, then went to visit with Jude. Wesley was doing well. He was taken off CPAP again for 2 hours last night.

He now weighed 1.487 kg, a gain of 8 g.

22 December 2006

Day 118 (40 + 2)

Wesley's due date. His nose was very sore, no swab taken, the cut on his nose is more prominent. The Nasal Septum had completely split. When he was on life support they used a hat to secure the tube, but CPAP doesn't have a hat attached, so they pulled it and made it too tight and that had split his nose.

He was being taken off CPAP for 1 hour twice a day and was tolerating it very well. They checked his stoma and it was intact. I felt strange about today being his due date. I just felt like crying all the time.

He now weighed 1.412 kg, a loss of 75 g.

23 December 2006

Day 119 (40 + 3)

I visited Wesley in the morning and evening and was told that he had lost more weight – how and from where, nobody knew. I thought there might be a problem with the bed scales, but they would not change them.

He now weighed 1.432 kg, a gain of 20 g.

24 December 2006

Day 120 (40 + 4)

I went to church and attended the love feast. It was nice to see everyone. I did not give my testimony, but I think I should have.

Wesley was fine in the morning, came off CPAP for 2 hours. His stoma was fine and his nose was getting better.

He now weighed 1.455 kg, a gain of 23 g.

25 December 2006

Day 121 (40 + 5)

We went to see Wesley early this morning. He was doing well; I cleaned his mouth and did his cares. He would come off CPAP later today. His cares were done at 12 pm and then he had to wait while his dummy was sterilised – he was so upset. Jude and I went to mum's house for Christmas dinner.

Wesley now weighed 1.453 kg, a loss of 2 g.

26 December 2006

Day 122 (40 + 6)

I left Jude at Mum's and spent the day dragging my feet and relaxing. Went to see Wesley twice; he was doing fine. On the last visit I felt like I was getting a cold and a cough, so I decided not to visit him for too long in the evening. Went to bed early.

I was not sure about his weight – it was recorded as 1.433 kg.

27 December 2006

Day 123 (41 + 1)

What a day! I called about Wesley: he could tolerate 2 hours off and 4 hours on, and during the ward rounds he did 3 hours on and 3 hours off. His weight was down yesterday, so I hoped that would improve later. Dad went to see him, and his stoma was fine, although it hadn't been checked.

He now weighed 1.47 kg, a gain of 37 g.

28 December 2006

Day 124 (41 + 2)

Wesley was now off CPAP for 3 hours and on for 4 hours and tolerating his feeding, which had gone up. He had a new incubator without weighing scales, so they were going to use digital scales. Wesley looked good after two days – I saw him in the morning and evening.

He now weighed 1.5 kg, a gain of 30 g.

29 December 2006

Day 125 (41 + 3)

Wesley was doing well; he was just being left to get on with it until he went for his operation. I changed his stoma bag with Corrin – it was very dirty.

His weight was up by a large amount and he was being weighed by the scales. He now weighed 1.73 kg, a gain of 230g.

30 December 2006

Day 126 (41 + 4)

I went to see Wesley today. He looked well and he had put on some real weight, I could tell. I held him for approximately 2 hours. He was crying because he was hot (37.2°C), but he picked up once I removed his blanket. He did 6 hours off CPAP.

He now weighed 1.82 kg, a gain of 90 g.

31 December 2006

Day 127 (41 + 5)

Wesley was being taken off CPAP for as long as he could tolerate it. He did very well today.

I went to church and prayed for my boys. I would also be visiting in the evening to bring in the new year and anoint both my boys with oil. We prayed with Wesley, and Jude held him for 2 hours; he fell asleep. Wesley did four and a half hours off CPAP.

He had not put on any weight, so he still weighed 1.82 kg. There was a problem with the scales again and all they said was, "We have changed them. They're different ones. This happens with different makes." I did not believe any of it; I just thought they weighed him with too much stuff in the incubator from time to time; this was a better explanation than *'the scales have changed'*, because the scales were within the incubator, so how could they be changed. What I realised then was that his weight depended on the person who had him for the night.

There had been a lot of change in Wesley over the previous couple of weeks – through his due date, Jude's birthday, Christmas Eve, Christmas Day and New Year's Eve. I had thought I would have my little man home by the end of the year, so it really made my heart ache that he was still in hospital, especially since several parents had gone home or were about to. We were still there, without an end date.

January

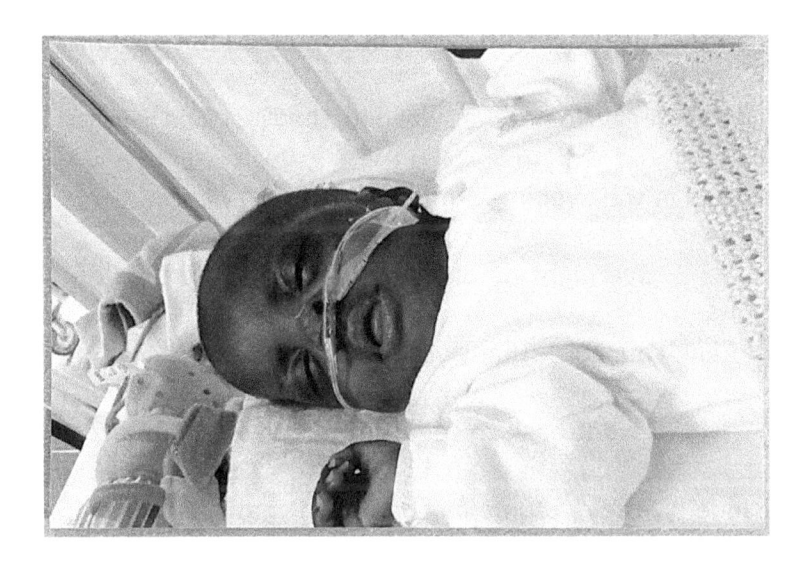

1 January 2007

Day 128 (41 + 6)

Wesley had his bag changed. His preemie clothes no longer fit so I bought him new clothes. OMG, my boy is growing!

"Have you seen the preemie clothes?" I said. "There is hardly anything of them".

The preemie clothes looked like badly made dolls clothes using left over pieces of material. I was glad I could now buy him real clothes because he had grown bigger.

I went to visit Wesley today with Jude and Trevor. Wesley was taken off CPAP, but he could not stand it for the whole time. No one was worried, they just said they would try again in the evening, but I began to worry again.

Overnight he did 6 hours off and 4 hours on. Wow! Thank you, Lord. Thank you, Jesus.

I went back to see in the new year with Wesley and Jude. Wesley's stoma bag had been changed twice in 2 days. It was concerning – one minute his bag was left until it fell off in my hand and the next they changed it nearly every day. It looked like it would need changing again soon because they did not know how to empty it without getting it dirty. Should I be worried?

The nurse said his nose had eroded – what did that mean? I had a look and they had been putting the CPAP on so tight that he only had one nostril; the part in the middle, the nasal septum had gone. That was worrying. I asked if he was in pain and how we were going to put the CPAP mask or cannula on, they did not give me an answer.

He now weighed 1.84 kg, a gain of 20 g.

2 January 2007

Day 129 (42)

Wesley had a good day. I enquired about his nose and they said the nurse was coming to see him tomorrow. His nose was looking very sore, but he needed to be on CPAP. They said they would take a picture, but no one seemed to be worried, or maybe they were just smiling to make me think that it was all fine, they would see what it looked like. The result of the Swab taken of his nose was not yet back.

I had a blood test and it was normal. They were checking to find out if there was something hereditary.

The nurses had a lack of understanding of the stoma. No one seemed to know what to do about the stoma – it was checked by the nurse and it was fine, but they just didn't seem to understand the stoma and what it meant.

He came off CPAP for 7 hours and was back on for 4 hours – well done, honey. He now weighed 1.85 kg, a gain of 10 g. I didn't know whether to accept the weight gains or pay no attention to them, because when I accepted them, the rug would get pulled from beneath me and we'd be back to square one.

3 January 2007

Day 130 (42 + 1)

They were not consistent with the times for taking Wesley on and off CPAP – what was going on? I thought maybe they were being cautious; there was no way to tell what they were planning. Wesley was taken off for 8 hours and put on for 4 hours and he did well. They increased the time they were taking him off – thank you, Lord. I was surprised at his oxygen requirement, 8-12%, but he was tolerating it very well.

I was told Wes, and I would be going to Addenbrooke's on Sunday 7 January to have his op on Monday 8 January. I did question if that was really going to happen; it had been cancelled before. I also wondered why they were so eager to get his stoma closed.

He now weighed 1.91 kg, a gain of 56 g. I wanted to scream with joy. *But is it going to change when they realise there was a rock in his incubator? I'm joking, but at this point how do I know what's real and what's not?*

4 January 2007

Day 131 (42 + 2)

Wesley came off CPAP at 3 am and was back on at 11 am. I was so proud of my little man – he looked so good, and his oxygen still looked good, on 8% after being on 3%.

I slept most of the day. Sometimes I felt so tired I couldn't keep my eyes open. Wesley did 8 hours off twice and did very well. He desaturated and sometimes his oxygen requirement went up to 30% by the end of his stint off.

He'd gained weight; they'd added powder to his milk for weight gain. He now weighed 1.93 kg, a gain of 24 g. I hoped the powder was working.

5 January 2007

Day 132 (42 + 3)

Wesley had a good night last night; everything was fine. He made me so proud. His stoma bag was changed yet again – I thought they were toying with me. Once his bag fell off because it was dirty, and now they kept changing it for no reason – I would have to discuss that.

He was now being taken off for 9 hours and put on for 3 hours, twice a day. He was off more than he was on. He would be transferred to Addenbrooke's on Sunday, if the bed was available – we had been disappointed before, so we just had to pray and wait. He would be transferred on CPAP, so why were we working so hard to get him off it? He would be on the ventilator for the op, then on continuous CPAP, then he'd have to be weaned off CPAP again. He was doing so well coming off that I would rather he came off CPAP then went to Addenbrooke's. They then changed it to 12 hours on and 12 hours off and 3 hours on. I would not have minded if our trip to Addenbrooke's got cancelled again, to be honest.

He now weighed 1.98 kg, a gain of 50 g. It looked like the weight gain was real. I had not had the speech about the scales being changed again, yet!

6 January 2007

Day 133 (42 + 4)

Wesley needed a blood transfusion tonight because his haemoglobin was low. Preemie babies do not have an endless supply of blood and it does not replenish as quickly as that of a full-term baby. They had to keep taking blood from his heel to check his oxygen levels because he was off CPAP for so long, so his oxygen requirement kept going up and he was unable to come off CPAP like he had been doing. I just felt that we had so much going on now, why didn't we just concentrate on one thing – getting him off CPAP? Why were we also getting him prepared for his operation?

His dad wanted to find a house so he would be nearer to us, and he chose to go to Wellingborough, so I did not see Wesley today because I was looking for a house with Trevor. I felt that I had let Wesley down – he was doing so well coming off CPAP, but I just had to put his dad first and I felt so guilty about it. I feel that if I had gone to see him, what happened might have been avoided.

He now weighed 2.04 kg, a gain of 60 g. At least his weight was going up.

7 January 2007

Day 134 (42 + 5)

We were waiting for a bed to become available at Addenbrooke's.

They'd had an emergency overnight, but maybe it was for the best – my boy was not happy.

Wesley did not go to hospital as he had an infection because his tube was not in properly. Why? They did it all the time, so why was it wrong this time? Why did I take the day off yesterday? The one day they did something different and everything fell apart for my little man. How I have cried over this day; the guilt is enormous.

His stoma bag had to be changed again. Why, what was wrong with it? They said maybe they needed to call the stoma nurse, maybe he needed new bags. He was now on 55% oxygen – that was high for him, but the nurse did not think it was a problem. He had put on weight though, so he now weighed 2.06 kg, a gain of 20g.

We'd had a strange couple of days. I asked God for help. Maybe the time was not right for the stoma reversal. Everything in God's time.

8 January 2007

Day 135 (42 + 6)

Wesley was supposed to have his stoma reversal today, but he did not go to Addenbrooke's, so the operation did not happen. He was unwell, but it was a good thing on this occasion; we would not be going to Cambridge until he was better.

I saw Wesley this morning, and he seemed to have a problem with his throat. The doctors did not think he had an infection, although I did because I had a throat infection and I had been holding him every day. They thought he needed mouth stimulation, I asked for a swab to be taken of his throat and to start him on antibiotics, to take cultures, the feeding tube could be used. I kept asking them to take a swab, not sure if they did as I stayed at home this evening with my throat infection.

He now weighed 2.08 kg, a gain of 20 g.

9 January 2007

Day 136 (43)

I decided to stay home as I had been diagnosed with a throat infection. I did not see Wesley today, but I did phone and ask for him to be taken off CPAP to avoid giving him a nose problem. I was not sure what had happened to the plastic surgery nurse, but they did take him off and found that he might have streptococcus, part of the cold family. They did not want to check, but they found what I'd said, so they started him on antibiotics: 500 mg amoxicillin. Thank God they started the antibiotics.

He had put on weight and seemed to be doing very well. He was being taken off CPAP for 2 hours, three times a day. He weighed 2.1 kg, a gain of 20 g.

10 January 2007

Day 137 (43 + 1)

Wesley was taken off CPAP for 3 hours from 2 pm to 5 pm. He handled it very well, oxygen 33–35%. I went to see him early and he looked lovely, but he was fast asleep. I so wanted to hold him and cuddle him and keep him safe. My little man, who could fit into my hand when he was born, was now looking like a baby.

His bag was intact, but they had not changed it again, for no reason. His nose was okay, as good as could be expected given that the mask was still being used. He was getting bigger, but he looked good with it. He was still on the regime of 2 hours off, 6 hours on.

He now weighed 2.146 kg, a gain of 46 g.

11 January 2007

Day 138 (43 + 2)

Wesley was doing well. He was coming off CPAP three times

a day for 2 hours at a time to rest his nose, so now there was a different reason for him to come off CPAP, but it was still going the right way. It was so irritating – we still did not know what the cultures showed.

Wesley looked so big when I saw him today, my gorgeous boy. I stayed away as I still had a throat thing, but I would visit again on Saturday morning. I hoped I would not need to be away from my little man for too much longer.

No bed at Addenbrooke's for Wesley. I was still praying and I knew this was best for him; the time would come and we would go.

He now weighed 2.152 kg, a gain of 6 g.

12 January 2007

Day 139 (43 + 3)

Wesley was doing fine. He was still on antibiotics, but his oxygen seemed quite high again. What was going on with him? No one seemed to know – despite the antibiotics, he still seemed unwell.

He was still off three times a day for 2 hours at a time, and he'd be on antibiotics till Sunday. Normally the first day of antibiotics brings a change, but he still did not seem his old self. From what the nurses were telling me, his cultures had come back. It was so hard not to feel guilty when every time I stayed away from him he got sick, or something went wrong. I stayed away too long, again – would I never learn? Depending on who was taking care of him, they let me know what type of care he would receive. I would go back tomorrow.

He now weighed 2.17 kg, a gain of 18 g.

13 January 2007

Day 140 (43 + 4)

I was told that the swabs from his throat had come back normal, but there was something going on. His saliva had not been sent off to be checked. Maybe they would do it now because nothing else was showing what was going on with my sweetpea. His oxygen was 55%, which was quite high. An echo would be done on Tuesday.

I saw Wesley for the first time this morning and held him and he just kept crying. He seemed to be very uncomfortable – he was never uncomfortable, he never cried in pain, he had a high pain threshold. *Lord, please lead the doctors to what is ailing him.*

He now weighed 2.192 kg, a gain of 22 g.

14 January 2007

Day 141 (43 + 5)

This morning Wesley was looking very lethargic. His eyes looked dull and he seemed to be in pain. I touched his side and he seemed to grimace. 45–50% oxygen. The nurse spoke with the doctors on their rounds and they did an echo: his feeding tube was too low. Why hadn't they checked the tube before? They always did, but I was not around so they had treated my son like a piece of meat. To me it seemed like they just had him on a conveyor belt for treatment that might cause him discomfort, the feeding tube was then made shorter by pulling it back up. Saliva was taken, an echo was done, but they showed nothing obvious and nothing changed. He was put on erythromycin (an antibiotic) for respiration.

He now weighed 2.27 kg, a gain of 78 g.

15 January 2007

Day 142 (43 + 6)

Wesley was on 45% oxygen. A few days ago, this would have been too high, but he was coming down off higher – he had an infection again, after all. His oxygen requirement was going down, yes, thank God. Also, he was on CPAP for 8 hours, but let's change the narrative, let's call it CPAP and cannula, off CPAP, 2 hours on the nasal cannula.

He was getting frustrated because he needed mouth stimulation. Why did everything take so long? Why did I keep asking for help for my son and getting a delayed response? He was still not my child and he wouldn't be until I had him home – then these people would have to listen to me. I was having a meeting with his consultant tomorrow and I would bring a new dummy for Wesley then.

He did his 2 hours off CPAP (on the cannula) and I put some milk on his dummy. Up until then, Wesley had been tube fed – fed like a fatted calf so he would put on weight. Now he needed to take a bottle. *Lord, help the nurses and doctors realise that he needs to take a bottle.* They were so fixated on closing his stoma at Addenbrooke's that they were not looking at the other things he now needed.

He now weighed 2.31 kg, a gain of 40 g. That is an acceptable weight for a child born early; If he had been born at this weight, it would have been considered normal. So many things remind me of what could have been, what *should* have been, if I had not travelled, maybe. Hindsight is a wonderful thing. I did come back from the holiday relaxed, but then I was stressed because my little man came too early.

16 January 2007

Day 143 (44)

Wesley was frustrated and needed to be held more. He was behaving like a new-born. He did not want to lie down all the time; he wanted to be in the arms of his mum or his brother. He was behaving like a full-term baby. He was also making sucking movements with his mouth – another thing that made him frustrated because he needed to be fed through his mouth.

35% oxygen: lower again. The antibiotics were working so he needed less oxygen. The cardiologist saw Wesley and said we would expect the hole between the left and right ventricles of his heart to close by itself, (not to be confused with the PDA which was outside the heart). Was this something else I needed to be worried about? The heart is one of the main areas of the body that needs an eye kept on it.

The Neonate consultant would be coming to see Wesley more. They said we now needed to establish hourly feeds and do more time off CPAP. The Speech and Language Therapist came to see Wesley, they also said they had to check him for brittle bones.

I requested a meeting with the consultant to ask about giving Wesley bottle feeds and whether he could go into a cot, but my chat with the doctor was hijacked by Trevor. He stayed away all the time, yet he still wanted to call the shots. The doctor took me to places I was not really interested in going. We had someone in the room taking notes and she went through Wesley's whole file. I kept wanting to ask what she was doing, but after she had gone through his file and told us things I did not want to know about, she asked me if I had any questions.

I said, "All I want to know is can Wesley go into a cot now?"

She looked at me. "His dad said you wanted to know everything that was being done."

"I only want to know about bottle-feeding and if he can go in a cot. His dad is the one who needs to know everything. I am quite happy to leave everything like it is."

So, Wesley was put in a cot and I was very happy.

He now weighed 2.326 kg, a gain of 16 g.

17 January 2007

Day 144 (44 + 1)

I decided to buy Wesley a mobile that played classical music for his cot. He was tolerating hourly feeds, and they would probably change to 2 hourly feeds tomorrow. I also bought him a rattle that he seemed to like, and a different dummy with a smaller teat. I was not sure if I wanted him to have a teat, but I thought it would be more for mouth stimulation than anything else.

He was outgrowing his clothes. He now weighed 2.366 kg, a gain of 40 g.

18 January 2007

Day 145 (44 + 2)

Wesley was now being fed every 2 hours. That doesn't sound like a big deal, but he was no longer being fed like a fatted calf; he was being fed like a normal baby.

When I did his cares, I noticed that the bag would need changing soon. They had stopped changing his bag for no reason, so at least things were settling down. I would do it very soon, possibly tomorrow.

His oxygen was going up and down – not sure why, but whatever Wesley needs and wants, he gets. The transfer to Addenbrooke's for the stoma reversal had been scheduled again for 5th February, with the operation on the 7th of

February. By the grace of God, we would go then; it seemed to be what the hospital was concentrating on.

He now weighed 2.52 kg, a gain of 154 g.

19 January 2007

Day 146 (44 + 3)

Wesley was now on feeds every 3 hours and again he was doing well. He got a bit restless as his tummy was getting full, and I was a bit concerned as he then came off CPAP for 3 hours. Was that a good thing? His gases were fine and he seemed to be tolerating it well. Who knew? Obviously not me.

He seemed to enjoy his mobile, the music was all classical. I was always praying and anointing Wesley with olive oil, and there were several nurses who would pray with him when I was not around and during the night. I changed the stoma bag.

He now weighed 2.555 kg, a loss of 15g. His weight loss always seemed to coincide with him coming off CPAP.

20 January 2007

Day 147 (44 + 4)

Trevor came round today and we went to Northampton to look at houses. It gave me some time away, but I missed Wesley so much I wanted to go back very quickly.

I saw Wesley in the morning and he was doing fine, no changes. Although he was tolerating his feeds, he needed to see the SALT nurse to talk about mouth stimulation. It was all very well bulk feeding him, but part of his speech would come from being able to move his mouth. He wouldn't be able to form words otherwise.

The SALT nurse saw Wesley in the evening. He was asleep and looked fine. To be honest I was not sure what she recommended for Wesley. He was asleep so what could she see or check? Some things on this journey gave me more questions than answers, so I just went with the flow. To speak, Wesley would have to be alive and breathing by himself – that was the priority for now.

He was still doing 3 hours off, 6 hours on. Trevor came to see him. He always looked so out of place, never relaxed, and he made me feel like I needed to make excuses and we always left quickly. Thank you, Lord.

Wesley's bag was changed this evening. He now weighed 2.538 kg, a gain of 33 g.

21 January 2007

Day 148 (44 + 5)

I went to see Wesley this morning. I went by myself even though his dad had stayed at our house. It was strange – he had all these excuses about why he couldn't visit too much. He waited at home for me to come back before he left to go home.

I had felt very upset for the past 2 days. CPAP was probably a factor, otherwise I'm not sure why. Maybe I was expecting Wesley to be off CPAP more, to be making more progress. He seemed to take two steps forward and one step back. *He is in your hands, Lord, do your will.*

I saw him this evening, no changes to report. His bag was changed by the nurse as it was leaking. I think they needed someone to tell them how to change the bag; it happened too often. He now weighed 2.626 kg, a gain of 88g.

22 January 2007

Day 149 (44 + 6)

I dropped Jude at the bus stop then went to see Wesley. He was awake and I stayed with him until the doctors did their rounds. The SALT nurse would visit today, and a stoma nurse to check the bag was intact.

The SALT nurse advised we bottle-feed him, so Wesley was given his first bottle today by his brother Jude. He took all 66 ml. Well done, honey. I really wanted to breastfeed him, but now I wouldn't get the chance. Wesley fell asleep in Jude's arms, and while he was asleep I took a lovely picture of them together.

He now weighed 2.624 kg, a loss of 2 g.

23 January 2007

Day 150 (45)

Wesley was doing fine; I saw him this morning. He came off CPAP for 5 hours and his stats were taken almost 2 hours later. I questioned whether they could get a proper reading 2 hours after he went back on CPAP and they said yes, it was good. How did that work? I did not understand, even after it was explained to me; surely his pointers would be good if he had time to take the oxygen from CPAP?

I changed Wesley. Jude was off school because of snow so we were going to spend time together. We went to the hospital in the afternoon and I gave Wesley his first bottle.

He got tired – he used a lot of energy, not to mention oxygen, trying to breathe and drink at the same time.

Not sure about his weight, but I think it was 2.5 kg.

24 January 2007

Day 151 (45 + 1)

Wesley did fine today. Although he came off CPAP for 4 hours and 5 hours yesterday, today he could only manage 4 hours and his gases were not very good. The staff were inconsistent with when they checked his gases, the time he came off CPAP and how quickly he was put back on, and what they did when his oxygen was coming up. I spoke to the sister about consistency and she defended something that did not need defending. *God, please help me to be more tolerant.*

I wasn't sure if he had lost or gained weight - I was losing count as there were other things happening now, but he weighed 2.624 kg again. He had been this weight twice over the past few days, so I wondered if they were weighing him at all.

25 January 2007

Day 152 (45 + 2)

Wesley was coming off CPAP twice a day for 4 hours. He did not seem to be able to handle much more than this. He was also taking his bottle, but there was no regime, no consistency, and that worried me.

Wesley had discharge out of his anus and no one could honestly tell me why. *Lord, tell me what to do.*

Jude said, "I have been an only child for 12 years, so now it's Wesley's turn to have my care and home." I remember thinking that was a random statement at the time.

His weight was now 2.568 kg; it seemed to have gone down.

26 January 2007

Day 153 (45 + 3)

I wanted to know if Wesley could take a bottle with less in it, as he got very tired from a full one. I just wanted him to be well for his op. I argued with the nurse about his feeding tube. I was feeling very anxious, and I even cried while expressing milk.

Wesley turned 5 months today and there was a lot happening. I gave him his first bath – it was scary, but I was so happy to be doing something normal with my son. The nurse who helped me seemed to be the only one who understood and knew what to do with this stoma. She said it was a bum on his tummy, so it had to be washed and treated as such, so we took the bag off and gave him a nice bath. We washed behind his ears and under his neck.

Daisy looked after him today. He now weighed 2.602 kg, a gain of 34 g.

27 January 2007

Day 154 (45 + 4)

Wesley still had a very high oxygen requirement. When this happened, he needed to either go back onto CPAP because he had an infection brewing or have a blood transfusion. *Why, Lord, is there no explanation from the doctor?* The doctors were trying to work out why his oxygen was so high. He was probably going to start using a nebuliser to clear his bronchioles and open his airways. *I am waiting on you, Lord.*

He now weighed 2.678 kg, a gain of 76 g.

28 January 2007

Day 155 (45 + 5)

Wesley started the nebuliser. He seemed to enjoy it – really enjoy it. In this misery, I was looking for joy in the weirdest places. 12–6–12–6 on and off CPAP, and my little soldier seemed to be okay with it. *Lord, it is in your hands.* I remembered the miracle that was Wesley and I knew that

God was bringing him through time. You cannot rush the Lord; He does things in His own time.

He now weighed 2.726 kg, a gain of 48 g.

29 January 2007

Day 156 (45 + 6)

Wesley was chilled again, which makes it sound like he was lounging on a beach somewhere, drinking a piña colada. He was using the nebuliser and handling it fine; he was off CPAP for 6 hours and on again for 6 hours, and he was happy with this. They did a review at handover. He was taken off CPAP and was able to manage seven and a half hours. Well done, sweetpea.

He now weighed 2.798 kg, a gain of 120g.

30 January 2007

Day 157 (46)

Wesley was doing okay. He had put on 72 grams overnight,

and although he looked well, his oxygen had been steadily rising. *Why? What is happening, Lord?* It was so hard to watch him go up and down on oxygen. What was happening to him? I had only held him for a short while without anything covering his face. His nose was very fragile from the CPAP. The doctors did not know, and neither did we, why Wesley was so oxygen dependent, Lord help him. 54% was very high. *Please help him, Lord God Almighty.*

He now weighed 2.784 kg, a loss of 14 g.

31 January 2007

Day 158 (46 + 1)

Wesley lost weight last night – only a small amount, but enough for me to mention it. Trevor came to see him tonight and cleared his mouth. Wow! It was a big deal because he had never touched Wesley until that moment. He had also bought a house in Wellingborough to be nearer to Wesley. I questioned this as he had only been to see Wesley a handful of times; At first I thought it was to be nearer to Wes, but I think he wanted to keep an eye on me as he said he didn't want anyone around his son.

Lord, his oxygen was still high. Where was the joy? Wesley was the joy and having my family around me was the best thing. He was having the nebuliser again, so maybe the joy was me seeing something new and thinking that it explained why he needed oxygen and why it was taking so long for him to come off CPAP. *Lord, when will his oxygen requirement go down? If he is not meant to have the op next week, so be it. It is in your hands, Lord.*

He now weighed 2.85 kg, a gain of 74 g.

February

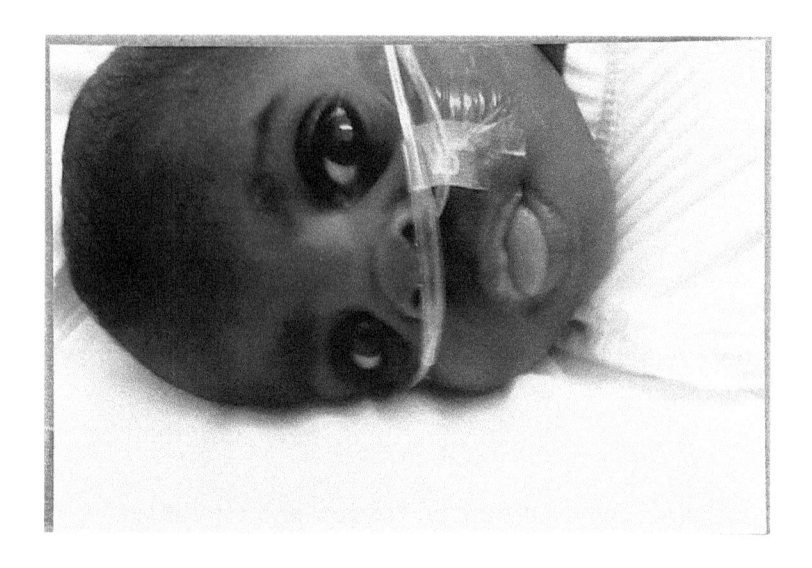

1 February 2007

Day 159 (46 + 2)

Wesley was doing well, although his oxygen level was still very high. The nebuliser was still being used and he was off for 6 hours and on for 6 hours. The nurse looking after him was different again. His treatment was inconsistent, this new nurse had dropped the nebuliser on the floor and proceeded to pick it up and use it on Wesley. However, this was never done for fear of infection. She also went to feed him without checking whether the feeding tube was in the right place.

Wesley was not very lively. *God, I hope he is not coming down with something.* He took his bottle.

He now weighed 2.92 kg, a gain of 62 g.

2 February 2007

Day 160 (46 + 3)

So today was a bad day. There was no organisation around when his bottle feed should be. It was far easier to feed him by the tube, so no one was concerned.

I went to see Wesley in the morning and the evening. His oxygen requirement was up at 7 pm and he still had not had even one bottle. I gave him a bottle when he was just off the cannula and he needed 1 litre of oxygen. Why?

They said they would try to take him off CPAP for 8 hours this evening, but they weren't sure if it would work as his oxygen requirement was very high. He had put on weight, so he now weighed 2.99 kg, a gain of 70g.

3 February 2007

Day 161 (46 + 4)

This was a day of *No, what happened?* It was the worst day I had with Wesley on the unit. I was told he had not handled being off CPAP yesterday; his oxygen was at 75%. What was going on?

I visited Wesley and he was in distress. He had been taken off CPAP while he was distressed and then rushed back on. My wishes had not been relayed by the previous nurse, and the nurse did not listen to me when I said "He seems unwell" before I went home. The relief doctor fiddled with Wesley's pressures – why? No blood gases were taken, no observations, no oxygen check, no interest in the welfare of any of the children – what happened?

He had put on weight, so he now weighed 3.02 kg, a gain of 30 g.

4 February 2007

Day 162 (46 + 5)

I decided to keep recording Wesley's weight, but not to document whether he had lost or gained weight. He was a good weight right now. Again, *what happened?*

Wesley had to be sedated because he was so tired. *Why* was he tired? Who was looking after him? Days like this were so overwhelming for me. I had watched little ones who were smaller than Wesley come onto the unit, be looked after better than Wesley and then get to the point where they were nearly ready to go home. When things like the past two days happened, I had to ask myself what was going on and whether I trusted anyone.

I spoke to Dr Oscar. I said I was not happy, I felt let down and I would have to spend more time here because I needed to keep an eye on the people who were looking after Wes, including the nurse assigned to look after him. I cried all morning for Wesley – if only the sister had taken me seriously, maybe he would not have been in crisis.

My Mum and Aunty Afa saw Wesley today. He had grown so much since they last saw them. His weight was now 2.92 kg.

5 February 2007

Day 163 (46 + 6)

Wesley's operation at Addenbrooke's was cancelled. I was not surprised – he was not well enough again – but I did not mind. They were placing a lot on his stoma reversal, like it was going to solve everything.

Nebulisation was a lot of nonsense. Again, there was a lack of consistency about giving Wesley the nebuliser. What a palaver! I told the nurse to forget the nebulisation. She was going to use it on Wesley after it dropped on the floor, and when she got a new one she could not work it. *What was going on?* I had to stay until 8 pm to ensure they used the correct procedure. I felt like screaming.

He was taken off for 1 hour. He now weighed 3.01 kg.

6 February 2007

Day 164 (47)

I decided to start writing down the name of the nurse assigned to Wesley in the morning and evening, after what happened a few nights ago, so many things went wrong and Wesley was in so much distress the locum doc nearly got my fist. I thought it was necessary. So, Angela (am) and Sam (pm).

His oxygen was down and there was a competent nurse looking after Wesley, thank God. What a difference the nursing staff make if they are competent! Although Wesley was settled all day and I was even able to give him a bottle, they did not allow him to come off CPAP. Angela realised I was upset and so she had a talk with the Sister and the Manager.

7 February 2007

Day 165 (47 + 1)

Wesley's operation day at Addenbrooke's was cancelled again. I felt good about it – the time was not right. I was still praying, and every time he went to have a procedure I felt good about it, but this one did not make me feel happy.

He was looked after by Angela and Angel. When I walked in I was pleased to see that Angela was looking after him. Thank you, Lord. The nurses from the Philippines were so much nicer and more mothering than the English nurses; they prayed with Wesley and with me.

I had a long talk with the manager and made a formal complaint. I hoped an incident like this would not happen again, but I would be there – my feelings were really messed up about his care. *Lord, I am waiting on you. Thank you for Angel tonight. She really knows what she is doing and Wesley is very well cared for.*

His oxygen was down to 44%. He was cuddled by the nurses looking after him tonight; I love my boy. I had a good night's sleep and his dad stayed over, it did not relax me, I am still feeling anxious. When he came off CPAP again, we were back there again: 1 hour on, 7 hours off. He now weighed 3.02kg.

8 February 2007

Day 166 (47 + 2)

Wesley was fine overnight; he was on the nasal cannula and he was now doing less than 2 hours off and 6 hours on. I took an old bouncy seat in for him to try when he was more awake. I wasn't sure if I should buy him a new one – was I scared to do so? I had not bought a cot or a highchair. I had just bought him some Babygro's, but I hadn't even bought him day clothes. The list went on.

He was allowed to have his bottles when he was awake and needed them, and after the past few days I thought everyone was being more attentive. They were taking it slow and being careful.

Wesley's oxygen had been steadily going down and he was doing fine. He tolerated 2 hours off very well today and I did not feel as anxious as I had been about the people looking after him. *Just relax and take it easy.* I felt that there was no rush, and the powers that be felt the same. The nurses looking after Wesley were competent, which meant I got a good night's sleep.

He was looked after by Angela (am) and Catherine (pm). He now weighed 3.12 kg.

9 February 2007

Day 167 (47 + 3)

Jude was off school again today. He went with Melvin, his best friend, so I spent the day with Wesley. The physio came by and showed me how to position Wesley in his chair. Why didn't I buy him a new chair? They make them so much better nowadays, but I just could not bring myself to tempt fate – it was bad enough when I had to buy him clothes. After, I went to pick Jude up.

Wesley came off for 3 hours and he did well. Changes were taking place slowly. Jude did his cares and he tolerated his bottles: one at 7 pm and one at 4 am. Nadia said he was fine overnight.

He was looked after by Sadie (am) and Nancy (pm). He did 3 hours off and 5 hours on. He now weighed 3.174 kg.

10 February 2007

Day 168 (47 + 4)

I saw Wesley in the morning. He was doing fine – more cuddles and bottles given. Julie was very busy today. If I had not been there, Wesley would have desaturated all the time. His CPAP machine kept losing pressure; I thought he needed a new one. There were new admissions all day.

Mary Jane was able to take Wesley off for 4 hours, on for 4 hours. I had a fair night's sleep, Wesley was okay.

He was looked after by Julie (am) and Mary Jane (pm). 3 hours on and 5 hours off. He now weighed 3.23 kg.

11 February 2007

Day 169 (47 + 5)

Wesley's regime had been changed again: 4 hours on, 4 hours off and he was tolerating it well. He sat in his chair for an hour and a half today. The sister thought he should stay in his chair longer because he needed more stimulation.

The night staff did not seem to get on with me. I could imagine people were a bit jumpy around me – after all, I had convinced the manager that one of the nurses should not be allowed to look after my son. I said if she was assigned to Wesley, I would be in the hospital all night watching her.

Charlotte, not one of the regular nurses, wanted to feed Wesley a bottle that had been standing for over half an hour. It didn't happen because I would not allow it and they would not go against me, so they made him another bottle.

He was looked after by Nancy (am), who had to spend a lot of time with him because there was a lot going on, and Charlotte (pm). He now weighed 3.29 kg.

12 February 2007

Day 170 (47 + 6)

Wesley spent the day with Macey; he did well. She noticed that he had bad gas from the previous night, which I was not told about. Is it wrong of me to say the nurses from the Philippines were more caring and attentive?

He had a good day and was monitored closely by his nurses. He had a good night with Angela, she felt that he needed to spend the time on CPAP. She made a good choice; he seemed to be overtired.

He was looked after by Mandy (am) and Angela (pm). He now weighed 3.332 kg.

13 February 2007

Day 171 (48)

He was looked after by Gemma and Rochelle (am) and Carol and Liz (pm). I don't know why he was with four people today; I can only think they were supporting each other or training new staff.

    Gemma did a good job, although I felt she did leave him in his chair too long – over 4 hours. Would you normally leave a child in a chair for over 4 hours if they were at home? When she tried to feed him, he was upset – of course he was, his body probably felt uncomfortable. Gemma gave him a bottle on two occasions. In the night I weighed him with Carol and he was sick all over me and the floor, but I saved his clothes.

    He now weighed 3.352 kg (7 lb 6 oz), a good weight.

14 February 2007

Day 172 (48 + 1)

Wesley's oxygen requirement was coming down. Thank you, Lord. I hoped there would be some changes made today. *Lord, what is wrong?* I needed to take a step back and hopefully that would help me see clearly. I cried for my boy today – not sure what to do, I felt driven to distraction.

Wesley had the first of his vaccinations and this gave him a temperature. I see people questioning vaccinations, parents refusing them and wanting their children to fight off infections, but we did not get a choice – our children were sick and so they had to take anything that was offered and we could not do anything about it.

My manager at work, Paul Jenkins, visited today, he said, he felt broody, and I had to question this. He walked onto the neonatal unit, saw all the sick babies with their machines beeping and he did not get it. He thought everything was cute, like he was on the maternity ward with full term new-born babies and happy parents and visitors, I found this shocking. I was later to find out he did not care; he came with an agenda that had been written by the company; They wanted me out.

Wesley was looked after by Angela (am) and Nell and Rochelle (pm). He now weighed 3.38 kg.

15 February 2007

Day 173 (48 + 2)

Wesley's temperature was down. He'd had a good night; he'd been weighed and had his cares done. They were still only taking him off for an hour at a time, so I hoped that would increase.

My feelings were still really mixed up and I was so angry. The health visitor convinced me that I was overreacting, as did all the medical staff. *Peace, Lord, help me to find peace of mind. Because right now that is not happening.* Of course, it was not happening – the shock of what I had seen and what had been done when I visited, and Wesley's distress, still haunted me, so if I was overbearing and annoyed, I would stand by it until I felt I didn't need to be any more. I felt like this situation had been created on the neonatal unit by some of the staff.

He was looked after by Kirsty (am) and Ann (pm). He now weighed 3.384 kg.

16 February 2007

Day 174 (48 + 3)

Wesley was settled overnight. I visited this morning and returned in the late afternoon. Jude came to visit in the evening. Wesley was doing fine. Jude held him and he loved every minute.

In the evening I breastfed Wesley. I cried a lot. I didn't feel like I could cope. There was so much going on, I was not sure how I was supposed to deal with everything. Work was getting on my nerves – after my manager visited, he started behaving like a prat and this was the first time I realised they wanted to take my job away.

Wesley was looked after by Julie (am) and Angela (pm). He now weighed 3.374 kg.

17 February 2007

Day 175 (48 + 4)

Wesley was looked after by Nell (am) and Rowena (pm) – very young ladies. Where was their experience? I went to see him on my own. He was unsettled in the morning: his bed was not right; his pressures were not right and he did not like the person looking after him. The nurses did not know anything about him. They told me, "Wesley wouldn't know the staff were inexperienced," but kids know. Why else would he be so unsettled?

I gave Wesley his bottle and when Rowena took over, I told her how I was feeling about him. I put him to sleep and came home, still feeling angry. When was I going to feel better about this? It was affecting me, I could not relax, but I needed to keep strong for Jude and Wesley. Wesley's hat was changed by Kirsty; he looked so cute.

    He now weighed 3.466 kg (7 lb 10 oz).

18 February 2007

Day 176 (48 + 5)

Kirsty had changed his hat again and it had marked his face. He had low oxygen with Tina, down to 43%; with Kirsty it was higher, 53%. Wesley was taken off CPAP at 6 pm for 2 hours, nebulised, fed and winded. He settled on my shoulder. Good gas. He started the regime again of 1 hour off a day – I wondered if he would make it this time.

    He was looked after by Tina (am) and Leslie (pm). He now weighed 3.526 kg (7 lb 12 oz).

19 February 2007

Day 177 (48 + 6)

Wesley was calm all through the night. He came off for an hour and a half this afternoon, 1–2:20 pm, and he did well. Still at 50% oxygen. Thank you, Lord.

Tomorrow we would see Philip Ink at Addenbrooke's to find out when Wesley would go there. He was coming off for 1 hour twice a day. He was doing so well and seemed to be handling his time off.

He was looked after by Nama (am) and Leslie (pm). He now weighed 3.596 kg.

20 February 2007

Day 178 (49)

Wesley had a good night. He had low oxygen while he was off CPAP and on CPAP, but we could always try again – Wesley is such a little fighter.

I spent the morning and early evening with Wesley and he was doing well, a lot better than before. He was back to a place where he was coming off more. Well done, sweetheart. He took all his bottle; he was putting on a lot of weight. He had a good evening, well settled.

He was looked after by Nama (am) and Leslie (pm). He was coming off for 1 hour three times a day. He now weighed 3.66 kg.

21 February 2007

Day 179 (49 + 1)

Wesley had a good night – he slept all through the night again for Leslie, like a full-term baby. He was seen by the physio and needed to have bloods taken. He was also going to be seen by the dietician because he was putting on too much weight. Really, that was so surprising – a few months ago we needed him to put on weight, and now we needed him to lose it. He came off nutriprem 2, which is full of calories, and was put on lower calories: duocal + sodium + mum (breast milk). He did well today. He tolerated his feeds, his time off, the nebuliser. Thank you, Lord.

He was looked after by Alison and Claire (am) and Tina (pm). He was still coming off for 1 hour three times a day. He now weighed 3.74 kg.

22 February 2007

Day 180 (49 + 2)

Wesley had a good night – although Tina was a bit scatty, she meant well. There were no changes during ward rounds (still coming off for 3 hours a day). *Lord, I will wait for you.*

There was confusion over nebulisation again: when would it be done and how? The night nurse had a different system to the day nurse. I questioned it and was made to feel that I was overreacting, but whenever they lacked consistency, things started to change and go wrong. I had to believe that God was in control.

He was looked after by Julie (am) and Rowena (pm). He now weighed 3.72 kg.

23 February 2007

Day 181 (49 + 3)

Julie said she did not feel that Wesley should come off CPAP anymore. *Why?* I did not get an explanation – that was why I was not happy when certain people were watching Wesley. What had changed?

They checked on his blood gases and the CO_2 had risen to 13, although he looked good when he came off the machine. He had a good day, although he got sick twice after his bottle.

He was looked after by Julie (am) and Diane (pm). He was still being taken off for 3 hours a day. He now weighed 3.668 kg.

24 February 2007

Day 182 (49 + 4)

Wesley had a good day. I was not feeling as anxious as I did before because I knew the nurses I liked had him and they were being extra vigilant. They didn't want to face the wrath of Cathy.

Wesley was taking his bottles and coming off CPAP, albeit for just an hour a day. He tried 2 hours, and after 1 hour his blood gases were good, so he did 2 hours. *Well done.* I was told he would be trialled on 2 hours twice a day.

I went to Sally's house and she was around to help me pray for Wesley.

He was looked after by Sam (am) and Bebe (pm). He now weighed 3.706 kg.

25 February 2007

Day 183 (49 + 5)

I felt anxious this morning. There still seemed to be anomalies with Wesley's care. *Lord, the devil has his people everywhere, please help me to fish them out.*

Sister Liz was the one on duty when Wesley got hurt.

Wesley seemed to be tolerating 2 hours off three times a day. Not sure this was accurate as a blood gas was not taken after the second hour. I felt that if they had taken a gas after 2 hours, then taking him off three times for two hours, we would know he was doing fine. Taking it after 1 hour I felt did not give a true reading of how he was doing.

He was looked after by Sam (am) and Ann (pm). He now weighed 3.78 kg.

26 February 2007

Day 184 (49 + 6)

Wesley had a good night. They were talking about reversing the stoma again, so we might have a bed at Addenbrooke's. He had been managing his 2 hours off three times a day. *Well done, babe.*

We got the bed in Addenbrooke's on the Paediatric Intensive Care Unit (PICU) as he was now too big for the NICU. We were just waiting for transportation. I left the hospital to go and rest, but I developed a headache because I had too much to think about. I kept thinking that my boy could survive with a stoma, but he couldn't survive without his lungs.

The transport team picked up Wesley at 9:45 am and arrived at Addenbrooke's at 10:45 am – he was well travelled! They didn't take his weight. *So, yet another hospital – let's see how we get on here.*

He was looked after by Sharon and Ann (am) and Rebecca (pm).

27 February 2007

Day 185 (50)

We were at Addenbrooke's. It was scary – it was so different and there were no shops to travel to.

He had a good night. Well done, son. The babies were weighed during the day. He was in an open cot and he seemed more settled. He needed a new hat for the CPAP. He was due to have the op on Saturday, but his lungs had to be checked first to ensure they were fine. By the grace of God, they would be. Again, new surroundings, new people, getting used to a new team. His bag was changed.

Wesley was looked after by Jemima (am) and Carol (pm).

28 February 2007

Day 186 (50 + 1)

I was now living in a cot next to Wesley's. The hospital bed was comfy and it felt like I was having a break. I had brought myself some packet noodles and Super Noodles.

Wesley had a good night. The difference at Addenbrooke's was they did not go into much detail, so you didn't find out too much. They weighed the babies on Monday, Wednesday and Friday.

Wesley had a good day. His oxygen went down to 45% for the day and it could have gone lower. He seemed to be enjoying himself. He took two bottles with no problem and he had his bag changed. No weight yet. Things had started up well, as they normally did in a new hospital.

March

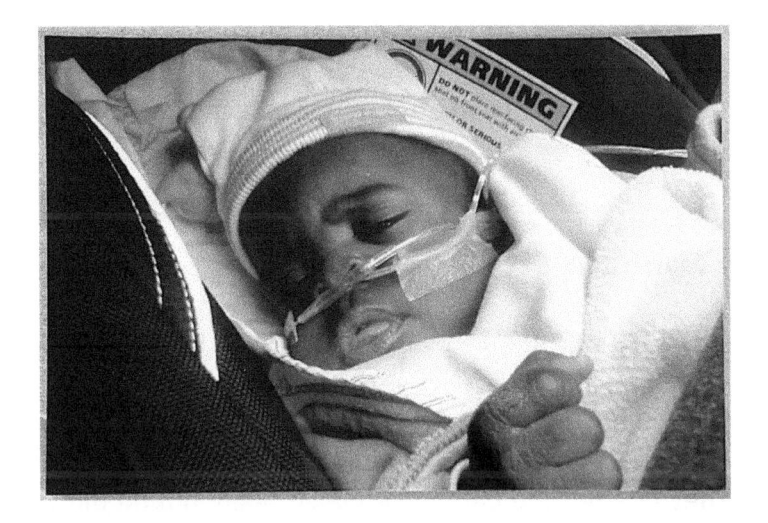

1 March 2007

Day 187 (50 + 2)

In this hospital it seemed that all the parents stepped up and looked after their own children. We were on the PICU, so the children were not critical, but we did get limited information.

He had a good night – very chilled out, no problems. I went home yesterday evening and planned to go in after 11 am this morning. Wesley was fine; he was being looked after by a posh (!) nurse. I felt anxious and out of place. Wesley was in yet another new place, but he was fine and he had travelled well. I hoped to see the resuscitation consultant tomorrow.

He was looked after by Valance and Paul.

2 March 2007

Day 188 (50 + 3)

Wesley had a good night, although he was sick a few times. They overfed the babies for weight gain, but he did well. He was very stable and slept right through.

I went to the hospital early as I had to see the resuscitation doctor. He said that Wesley had had a few setbacks – three, in fact, with his lungs. They were wet, with only a small part that appeared to be okay. The doctor said he would do a CT scan and a sweat test to rule out cystic fibrosis (that is not something people of colour get; our equivalent is sickle cell), and he said Wesley might grow out of the chronic lung disease by himself.

He was looked after by Valance and Paul. He now weighed 3.8 kg, up 18 g.

3 March 2007

Day 189 (50 + 4)

By the grace of God Wesley would grow out of the chronic lung disease; that would be one of the last hurdles in our journey. *All in God's time, we just must wait.*

Wesley had a good day. We got to the hospital at about 2 pm and left about 8 pm. He had a bottle at 6 pm. He was swaddled to stop him removing his CPAP. He looked so sad when he woke up. He slept on me, but I think he knew I was going because when I put him down, he kept waking up. I felt like a mum to Wesley today; it was even harder to leave him.

He was looked after by Leyla. He now weighed 3.95 kg, up 15 g.

4 March 2007

Day 190 (50 + 5)

Wesley had a good night, very stable; he did well. I went to church today, with the intention of not staying, but I got drawn in and stayed for two and a half hours. I felt good when I left with Jude – it was a good day.

One of the things that always happened when I came out of church was I would turn on my phone and there would be a message, but this time there were no messages, there was no anxiety. Praising God, I felt relaxed and in control.

Wesley was fed by Jude, winded and put down to sleep. He was looked after this evening by Billy. No weight was taken. His weight was good and every small increase was good, but it was an obsession. I realised that because his weight was taken every day in Luton, I felt sick when I did not have it while he was at Addenbrooke's.

5 March 2007

Day 191 (50 + 6)

Wesley had a good night, stable, no vomiting. His operation was cancelled as they needed to do certain tests beforehand, which wouldn't be done before Friday. I was still relaxed – all in God's time. He would choose the date and time.

Wesley was seen by the speech and language therapist, who was amazed at the speed with which he took his bottle and his recovery after; he was very well in himself. Addenbrooke's were looking at the areas of Wesley's body that he needed to survive. He could live with the stoma, but his lungs were very wet and they needed to be looked after too, and we needed to stop the repeated infections that had stopped him coming off CPAP.

He had his bag changed and was looked after by Nikki. No weight taken tonight, but it was not the most important thing – his weight was good.

6 March 2007

Day 192 (51)

Wesley had a good night, although he was sick because they force-fed him 85 ml.

All change: Wesley was going to have the sweat test, a contrast test and a CT scan tomorrow instead of Friday. They were also starting to arrange his bowel operation. Wesley had so much to go through tomorrow, I was going to make sure I was there with him, to keep him calm.

He had a very good day, saturating at 100% for quite a long time. I put him to sleep before I left. He was looked after by Nikki. I tried not to mention his weight loss/gain every day at Addenbrooke's.

7 March 2007

Day 193 (51+1)

Wesley had a good night; he did get sick after his last bottle.

All milk feeding stopped at 6 am in preparation for the operation on Friday; he would just be on a supplement until then.

I saw Wesley and he had his first rehydration treatment at 9 am. They decided not to proceed with the operation as they felt he might take a step backwards with weaning off the CPAP machine. He did not have the sweat test, contrast test or CT scan. I'm not sure who looked after him and he was not weighed. They gave him medication to try and get the water out of his lungs. To be honest, I was not sad about the operation not going ahead – all in God's time.

8 March 2007

Day 194 (51 + 2)

Because his operation had been cancelled, we were transferred back to the Luton and Dunstable Hospital today. Although I was upset about Wesley returning there, everything happens for a reason. I had learned a lot more about Wesley's care at Addenbrooke's and so I intended to highlight these things when he returned.

Wesley did well overnight and his oxygen level even went down to 38%. The last time he had achieved that was December, so he was doing very well. He was so full of his own personality. I had been treating him like a full-term baby and he made me smile.

Back in Luton I felt anxious. Wesley was put into an incubator as the isolation room was being used by someone else. I was upset he was in an incubator and more upset because one of the nurses thought it would be a good idea to put his music mobile in with him – really, it was too loud. Why was I back here?

He now weighed 3.9 kg, down 50 g. "Oh, it was the weighing scales, they have changed." Once again I had a question in my head.

He was looked after by Ann, Angel and Rena.

9 March 2007

Day 195 (52 + 2)

Wesley was getting hot in the incubator. His oxygen went down to 35% and he was saturating quite high. Still, he was amazing us all with his progress – last time he was in the 30% bracket was in December.

I disagreed with the Sister Nama about taking Wesley off CPAP. I explained to Dr Oscar and he understood. Why did I have a problem with Nama? Maybe it was because she said that the situation monitor was having difficulty taking Wesley's readings because his skin was so dark. *Please give me patience, Lord.*

We were looking at taking him off CPAP again, but he was in an incubator he was too big for, and because he had come from another hospital he needed to quarantine for a little while in the incubator.

He was looked after by Sam and Rachel. He now weighed 4.193 kg, up 293 g.

10 March 2007

Day 196 (52 + 3)

Wesley was now in a cot. He had a good night; his oxygen was 28–30%. The medication he was given for his lungs at Addenbrooke's seemed to have helped him. *We will see.* He did vomit, but that was nothing to write home about. He was still on all his normal meds.

He was taken off CPAP at 11 am for 1 hour and he did well, good blood gases. The plan was also to take him off at 11 pm. He had a good day. I went home in the afternoon and then returned. He tolerated his time off at night.

He was looked after by Sam and Rachel. He now weighed 4.08 kg, down 113g.

11 March 2007

Day 197 (52 + 3)

I went to see Wesley at 8 am. He was doing well. I changed his nappy and fed him. They were slowly taking him off CPAP.

I went home, then went into town to buy him some bits. I came back in the afternoon and gave him a good wash. I was now washing him more – he was quite big and he needed a bath or at least a sponge bath every day.

Oxygen 34%. He was now off for 2 hours at a time and tolerated it very well in the evening and tolerated all his feed. He was looked after by Linda and Daisy. He now weighed 4.138 kg, up 58g.

12 March 2007

Day 198 (52 + 4)

I came in to see Wesley at 11 am. He was doing well on the cannula, but he was not happy in his tummy. I fed him and noticed his bag was big, so I went to change it, but he got sick. I picked him up, at which point his bag popped and he vomited all over me (wonderful). My baby was doing baby things and it was so funny. I went home in scrubs.

His dad came up but did not visit with Wesley. His explanation: he did not want Wesley to get anything from him.

Wesley had a good night and was off CPAP for 2 hours twice today. He was looked after by Leslie and Angela. He now weighed 4.164 kg (9 lb 3 oz), up 26 g. I was back to obsessing about his weight.

13 March 2007

Day 199 (52 + 5)

Wesley had a good night. He tolerated his time off CPAP, which was good. His oxygen crept up a little bit, but it was nothing to worry about. I spent most of the afternoon at the hospital and then had to go and let Jude in – he was at football while I was seeing Wesley. We attended church for prayers in the evening.

Wesley went off CPAP for 2 hours three times today. He was looked after by Gemma and Caroline. He now weighed 4.216 kg (9 lb 5 oz), up 52 g.

14 March 2007

Day 200 (52 + 6)

Wesley had a good, settled night. He had put on a fair bit of weight, but I wondered whether he was retaining water. His alpha, one of the diuretics, had been stopped. I was not happy about that – he'd got these things at Addenbrooke's and they were working to get his lungs healthy.

Wesley has a good day. He was being trialled on a new regime and he seemed to be coping, although his blood gas did not show up very well. I was concerned that all the hard work that had been done at Addenbrooke's was going to be lost.

He was taken off CPAP for 2 hours twice and 3 hours once today. He was looked after by Kirsty, April and Candy. He now weighed 4.256 kg, up 40g.

15 March 2007

Day 201 (53)

Wesley had a good night, although he did vomit a lot with Candy. *What is going on, baby?* It might have been the move back to Luton.

He spent the day with Julie. She only had one other baby today and so she was able to spend a lot of time with him. He played a lot and spent time in his chair, which he seemed to enjoy.

He received his 200-day certificate. I was convinced that his 100 and 200 days had not been calculated properly. Being in isolation, we had space to play on the floor, which was welcome.

He was taken off CPAP for 2 hours twice and 3 hours once today. He was looked after by Julie and Teddy. He now weighed 4.23 kg (9 lb 5 oz), down 26 g.

16 March 2007

Day 202 (53 + 1)

Wesley had a good day and night. We were moved into the main area of the unit, which was not what I wanted – I felt safe in isolation, like we were working towards going home. Of course, this was not realistic. Wesley was still very sick, but in my head I was planning to go home.

There was a baby with MRSA who needed to be in isolation, so Wesley could not play on the floor as much, but that was fine, we made do outside. Yes, I had bought Wesley a pram. I hadn't thought this day would come! I hadn't bought anything when he was born; I was going to do it when I came back from Dominica. Then when I came back we were not sure if he would survive.

He was taken off CPAP for 2 hours twice and 3 hours once today. He was looked after by Julie and Jenny. He now weighed 4.252 kg, up 22 g.

17 March 2007

Day 203 (53 + 2)

I went to see my boy today. He still looked good coming off CPAP; he was doing okay.

We took Wesley for a walk outside in his new pram. When I went shopping for a pram I had to consider that Wesley would come home on oxygen, so I needed a pram with a place to put the tank when we went out. Surely one should shop for a pram that feels comfortable to push, with handles that are the right height. Not when you have a child who needs oxygen to breathe – I was learning something new every day. When we went outside for the first time, I could see that he was shocked, but I think he was still happy to be out. He had good gases and so we would see what happened.

He was taken off CPAP for 2 hours twice and 3 hours once today. He was doing well and we were all positive. He had come from Addenbrooke's and they were lung specialists, so they had done many things to help with his lung function. He was looked after by Kirsty and Angel. He now weighed 4.33 kg, up 78 g.

18 March 2007

Day 204 (53 + 3)

Wesley was doing well. It was very busy in the unit: there was a small new baby and the ward rounds were delayed because of it. I thought that these parents were just now starting their journey and they looked very scared to come into preemie world – we had all been there.

Dr Skinner felt that Wesley should be off CPAP for a bit longer, so his protocol was changed. I did not give him a bath as it was very busy. He was taken off CPAP for 3 hours twice today and 2 hours once. He was looked after by Nancy, Angel and Linda. He now weighed 4.4 kg (9 lb 11 oz), up 70g.

19 March 2007

Day 205 (53 + 4)

Wesley had a good night and had maintained his time off CPAP. I was so proud of him, but we had been here before and I was beginning to get anxious. I did this every time.

He had his sweat test for cystic fibrosis and he took it in his stride. I thought it might be a waste of time because it is very rare that a black person gets cystic fibrosis – we get sickle cell anaemia. He did very well and there was enough sweat for the diagnosis.

I did not see him this evening. Did I feel guilty? Yes because I would not be able to leave my child overnight once he came home. But I also felt happy with the people who were looking after him.

He was taken off CPAP for 3 hours three times today. He was looked after by Leslie and Jane. He now weighed 4.46 kg (9 lb 13 oz), up 60 g.

20 March 2007

Day 206 (53 + 5)

Wesley had a good night, and although I was told that he had good gases, I was still anxious about him coming off CPAP.

Part of the sweat test involved having a CT scan. Wesley went in an incubator to get to the scan and he was sedated. He was a bit big for the incubator now, but we managed. Wesley was well when he started coming round from the sedation, and I was able to hold him while we waited to be taken back to the NICU in Luton. Another test ticked off the list.

He was taken off CPAP for 3 hours three times today. He now weighed 4.479 kg, up 19 g.

21 March 2007

Day 207 (53 + 6)

Wesley had a good night, although his gases were not so good; he was only able to withstand 2 hours off the machine. As I said, my anxiety levels went up with every extra hour he was taken off CPAP. He seemed to have an infection again and I thought his time off would be changed again.

Wesley had a mixed day. I did not go to see him as I had a cold. His oxygen requirement had gone up and, looking at him, he seemed to be retaining water.

He was taken off CPAP for 2 hours twice and 3 hours once today. It had changed, but at least he was still coming off. He now weighed 4.506 kg, up 27 g.

22 March 2007

Day 208 (54)

Wesley had a good night. He took all his bottle and slept, although he was awake for quite a while.

He had an appointment to see Dr August but it had to be moved to another day because Wesley was not feeling well. Dr August contacted me – everything was in line with what they thought, but they would know more once Dr Ink at Addenbrooke's had a look. He was the lung specialist who had been helping Wesley; he had helped to clear his lungs when they were very wet and full of fluid.

Wesley had a good day; his sweat test was fine; it would have been a surprise if he had Cystic Fibrosis because it is not something that affects black people; He was taken off CPAP for 2 hours twice and 3 hours once today. He now weighed 4.478 kg, down 28g.

23 March 2007

Day 209 (54 + 1)

Wesley had a good night. I saw him today and for the first time, in a long time I felt a little bit anxious. He recognised me and when I picked him up, he vomited on me. I now had my thoughts confirmed, they were overfeeding the children to help them put on weight, and so when I picked him up the extra milk would just flow out of him. At the time I was concerned about his vomiting, although they did not seem to be.

I brought Jude to see Wesley today; he had been started on antibiotics. I loved seeing my boys together – they looked alike.

He was taken off CPAP for 2 hours twice and 3 hours once today. He now weighed 4.57 kg, up 92 g.

24 March 2007

Day 210 (54 + 2)

I could not visit today because I went to Blackpool. I did contact the hospital, but there were no changes during the rounds, although they were going to try and miss his feed at 3 am and compensate by adding milk to his feed during the day. He had a good day; his regime was still the same. They did a haemoglobin test, as well as bloods.

He was taken off CPAP for 2 hours twice and 3 hours once today. He was looked after by Julie. He now weighed 4.58 kg, up 10 g.

25 March 2007

Day 211 (54 + 3)

I was not able to see Wesley this morning – the clocks went forward an hour, so I missed my chance. They did not weigh him today; they missed it for some reason. When I saw Wesley, he did look well, but he seemed to be gasping. He was only off CPAP for an hour, but he seemed to be trying to clear his throat; he might have a cold. The doctor did an X-ray: Wesley was very sick and the suction they used was a kind of vacuum to clear a Childs throat if they are producing too much phlegm.

He was taken off CPAP for 2 hours twice and 3 hours once today. He was looked after by Victoria and Jade.

He now weighed 4.58 kg, no change from yesterday.

26 March 2007

Day 212 (54 + 4)

Wesley looked good this morning, but he was vomiting as he had a lot of wind. A cannula was put in for a possible blood transfusion, but after the ward rounds the cannula was removed – no transfusion needed. Preemies have collapsible veins, so it can take a long time to find a vein. I could not understand why they put Wesley through all that poking and bending of his hands and feet, twisting his legs, to put in a cannula just in case. Especially when it was removed within a few hours.

Wesley took his feed at 11 am very well, no vomiting. But he got sick whenever I went in today. He seemed to have a cold and was coughing a bit, then he got sick. He had a good evening, a good time off the machine, although he had a sore nose. I gave him a bath, which he enjoyed.

All through my journey with Wesley, we had found religious people working in the hospital who created a vigil around him and prayed when I was not there, they did this all the time; I felt blessed having nurses who understood.

I'm not sure how long he was taken off CPAP today. He was looked after by Jade and Angela. He now weighed 4.596 kg (10 lb 2 oz), up 16 g.

27 March 2007

Day 213 (54 + 5)

Wesley had a good night and during the day he did well. The doctor gave him his developmental test. They tested his hearing and his responses as best they could as he was born very early; we would have to wait and see what happened with him. He kept getting sick and the doctor said they would keep an eye on the vomiting and might reduce his feeds. His CT scan review had not come back yet. They did not record whether he was taken off CPAP – I'm not sure if he was. He weighed the same as yesterday, no change.

I was getting anxious about him, although I could not decide why. I think it was because we had come so far and we were so close to him coming home, but he wouldn't be allowed home while he was still on the CPAP machine, and his lungs were so bad they wouldn't reverse his stoma. I could deal with the stoma, but bad lungs meant that my boy was just being kept alive and it couldn't be sustained.

28 March 2007

Day 214 (54 + 6)

Wesley had a good night. He took his bottle off the ventilator – I wasn't sure whether that was a good idea or not, but we would see if there was any change during the ward rounds.

There was no change except that Wesley would now be weighed twice a week: Monday and Thursday. His time off CPAP was increased, same regime as before. Well, what was the regime? They were not telling me, or I was forgetting to write it down – either way, it is what it is. The CT scan review still had not come back. I thought they had put my son through the scan for no reason, just like they did when they put in the cannula. We would have to see what happened.

29 March 2007

Day 215 (55)

Wesley had a good night; nothing changed. He had his eyes checked and was signed off; there was no cause for concern there now. For one born so early, it surprised everyone that he did not have a problem with his eyes.

Wesley was very unsettled while he was off the oxygen; the lead that recorded his saturations was out. Also, Wesley's CPAP machine had no water in it, which caused him to be very dry. What was going on? They seemed to have lost the control around Wesley and now they were causing him pain. I felt like I was too outspoken and have mentioned it rather than created a fuss over it, I was calm about it, but wanted to know what they were doing about it. Why? Because we were so close and I thought they might do something to slow down his recovery.

We had to wait on the Lord, but as long as he was on the unit, he was not my son – he was a baby I had who had many mothers and fathers looking after him, and I was not one of them. Once I get my boy home, I would not bring him back into hospital, even if I had to keep him on me day and night to aid his recovery.

He was on the same regime, but there was no record of taking him off CPAP. I did not know how well he was doing; he was coming off CPAP, that was all I knew.

He was looked after by Sam. He now weighed 4.792 kg (10 lb 9 oz), up 196g.

30 March 2007

Day 216 (55 + 1)

Wesley had a good night. His machine was checked again and changed again. Why couldn't they find him a machine that worked?

He was doing well. Oxygen 50%, but not struggling. Normally he was on 35% when he came off CPAP, so I wasn't sure why it was higher, but the staff were not worried so neither was I – or so I tried to say to myself. He was on 30% oxygen when on the nasal cannula.

Wesley had a good day. I spent a good few hours with him and there were no changes on the ward rounds again, and no results from the CT scan. Where was Dr April? She had been gone for over a week. She was Wesley's consultant and she knew more about him than any of the others, but she was not around. Should I be concerned?

Same regime and he would not be weighed again until Monday.

31 March 2007

Day 217 (55 + 2)

Wesley was 14 weeks adjusted (adjusted age is the number of weeks since he was born minus the number of weeks he was early - so he was born 31 weeks ago, 17 weeks early). They kept adjusting his age because they said by the time he got to 2 years old they would know what was happening with him cognitively and be able to support him.

Wesley had a good night. He was very stable; he was on oxygen when he had his bottles. Anna was not very playful with him; she did not seem to know how to handle him. She was very capable of looking after him, I felt he was safe with her, but she did not play with or talk to him.

Wesley had a good day. I left the staff looking after him to update Anna about his time off. I did not record anything again because I had to go. I was trying not to be too bothered and then I wouldn't be disappointed when/if he did not come off the CPAP.

April

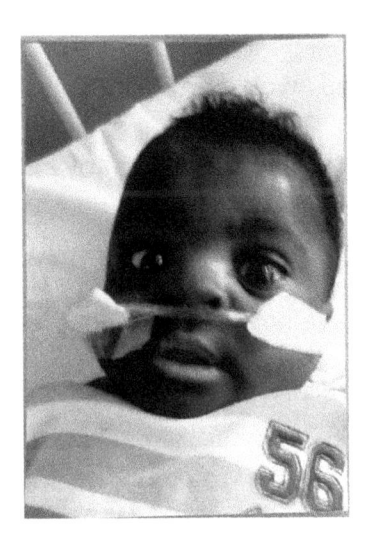

1 April 2007

Day 218 (55 + 3)

Palm Sunday, there had been so much happening, including a fair bit at home, but God is good and Trevor had to leave my house once his house came through. We had tried and tried to resolve the Child Support Allowance (CSA) issue, but he would not budge; he had made his plans. This was a man I had asked to marry me in December 2006, but now I saw a different side to him. He really was a horrible person. He had not grown up; everything was about him. At least Wesley was doing well despite his father's attitude towards me and Jude.

I decided I would not blame myself any more for what happened to Wesley – he came early and there were so many what-ifs. What if I had not travelled? What if Trevor had stopped me travelling? What if I had not got sick? What if I had left Dominica straight after the wedding? Would I have been saved from the E. coli? The thing is, hindsight is a wonderful thing, but it doesn't mean that nothing would have happened if I'd stayed in this country.

2 April 2007

Day 219 (55 + 4)

Wesley was being weighed today; I couldn't wait to see how he was doing. He now weighed 4.89 kg, up 98 g. His weight had really gone up, I was so happy. He was nearer to coming home. Thank you, Lord! Thank you, Jesus!

3/4 April 2007

Days 220/221 (55 + 6/7)

So, about the sperm donor, how would he deal with Wesley coming home. It's funny how you can be with someone and not really know them until you live with them. He always had to apportion blame to someone else and I put up with his whinging and wining. I do believe there was also another issue – a girlfriend – so did he feel bad? I don't think he did. He did not even feel guilty about spending time away from his son.

I prayed for his house to come through, please God. Trevor had been living somewhere but he had been thrown out. He said he was living with a guy, but his stuff was put in bin bags and thrown out – a woman's MO. He was in the process of buying his new house, and I couldn't wait for it to come through and for him to be gone.

We had decided to be there for Wesley, but he still wanted to come and stay whenever he wanted. We became a statistic. All the mothers of colour were always on their own in the hospital. The fathers were not present, but we supported each other at every hospital I went to. It was lonely and overwhelming, but we did not have time to melt down or cry; we had sick babies who needed us.

When Trevor went to visit Wesley on his own, the sister on the ward called me and asked what he looked like. She said she would sit with them to ensure he did not harm Wesley.

10 April 2007

Day 226 (56 + 6)

Wesley had a stoma because his bowel had disintegrated when he was 2 weeks old. The stoma was part of him; he'd only used his bum a couple of times. So, when I was changing him and I saw discharge, it was shocking. I told the staff – they did not think it was an issue, but I thought it was. I asked

Trevor to visit Wesley to talk about the discharge, but he refused.

Because of the discharge, I contacted Addenbrooke's and spoke to a lady called Andi, who contacted the NICU in Luton. Andi spoke with Dr Oscar at length about Wesley's progress: he was doing well and coming off the machine. He needed to grow out of the chronic lung disease, but he was doing well. This disease is not the same as adult chronic lung disease; it gets better in some preemies as they get older. I prayed that Wesley would grow out of it.

He was being taken off for 3 hours three times a day now, to be reviewed next week. I had finally been told the regime for getting Wesley off CPAP.

11 April 2007

Day 227 (57)

Wesley had been stable and his blood gases were very good, but I got a bit anxious about the discharge. Still no help from

Trevor; I would not update him about Wesley again. I was always on my own and I had to update my family about his progress, so why should I have to do that with his father too?

I took Wesley out for a nice walk around the grounds; he really enjoyed it. It was so good to have him in his pram and outside; it felt like we were going home soon. I decided not to talk about Trevor anymore – this day was about Wesley's journey.

12 April 2007

Day 228 (57 + 1)

Wesley was weighed today. I had a good few hours with him. I took him outside and he enjoyed it very much. He was putting on so much weight. Thank you, Lord. Thank you, Jesus.

He had a discharge again, which was sent off for analysis. His oxygen kept going down, but he was improving slowly. God bless Wesley.

He now weighed 5.2 kg (11 lb 7 oz), up 408g. His weight was going in the right direction.

13 April 2007

Day 229 (57 + 2)

Wesley had good gases yesterday and he had a good night – well done, Wesley.

This morning it was decided that he should be off for 4 hours, but only if I was there to look after him. He did very well; he had good gases and so would now be doing 4 hours off. He had a good evening. I gave him a wash, which he enjoyed. We had a cuddle and then I came home.

14 April 2007

Day 230 (57 + 3)

Wesley slept well. He had a good night, no vomiting. He played with his nurse and had a restful night.

Again, my weekend and week were taken over by problems with Trevor. He went away for the weekend but did not tell me – what a positively awful week.

15 April 2007

Day 231 (57 + 4)

God, I must offer You thanks. Wesley is stable and happy and doing good things by Your grace. He would be home soon. Always wait on the Lord, for He is good.

19 April 2007

Day 235 (58 + 2)

I spoke to Dr April. She was pleased with Wesley's progress but wanted to push him a bit more to see if he could come off for longer. We just had to wait on Wesley and the Lord. We could talk about going home, but the Lord needed time to do his work.

20 April 2007

Day 236 (58 + 3)

Wesley had a good day. He had good gases after his 5 hours off, but we needed to keep checking them. I noticed that Wesley seemed to be struggling; he seemed to have a cough and his oxygen had gone up a bit. No one seemed to be concerned, so we would just wait and see.

He was taken off CPAP for 5 hours twice and 4 hours once today.

21–23 April 2007

Days 237–239 (58 + 4–6)

Again, I did not write in my diary for a while – there were so many things happening, but nothing major with Wesley. I was still taking him out, which he seemed to enjoy. The only thing was that his oxygen had increased and he also seemed to have a cough/cold, but the doctors thought it was because he had been pushed too far, so they took an X-ray of his lungs, started antibiotics and did bloodshot checks – meaning they took some blood using a tiny straw. Preemies blood did not have time to regenerate as they had to take blood so often to check gas levels and various other things, so it was called blood shots, a shot of blood or an injection.

How did I feel? Every time we made progress, we took a step back. I felt like I was in turmoil and I was not sure what to do.

Wesley was still being taken off for 4 hours, although he had an episode today where he coughed so much that he was unable to clear whatever was in his throat. He had to be put back onto continuous CPAP. A secretion sample was taken and sent to be checked; he was still on antibiotics.

24 April 2007

Day 240 (59 + 1)

Wesley was really struggling; he had a cold. Another sample was taken. He was seen by the stoma nurse to check the sore around his stoma. She said his stoma looked healthy and clean. She changed the bags that he had to use. He was struggling with the cold. *God, help Wesley get over the cold.*

He now weighed 5.65 kg, up 450g.

25 April 2007

Day 241 (59 + 2)

Wesley was back on the big monitor as his saturation levels had decreased and they wanted to check it. He was coughing out very thick secretion – we would see what he was like after the ward rounds.

Wesley's oxygen went up to 100% for most of the day, so they tried him on a different machine with a mask on his face. It did not help; his blood gases were very bad.

26 April 2007

Day 242 (59 + 3)

Wesley had now been put onto BYPAP ventilation (a grey

machine). Although his oxygen was high, his blood gases were improving, but they might change during the ward rounds.

Wesley was now on 94% oxygen. His pressures on BiPAP were 7 (high) to help him breathe. Finally, it was established that he had a cold. All his pointers showed that there was no infection. Thank God.

It was a really harrowing day – just when I thought he would be coming off again very soon, he caught an infection. He was looked after by the nurses from the Philippines. They refused to put him back on life support and instead they held the oxygen over him. In the evening we all prayed around Wesley's cot and the nurses kept praying with him overnight. When I went in the morning his oxygen requirement had gone down.

27–29 April 2007

Days 243–245 (59 + 4–6)

Wesley was saturating well now, although he was still on high oxygen and he might also be teething. He had a good night, but he was unsettled for about 45 minutes in the morning.

My emotions were up and down, although I did believe that Wesley would pull through. I prayed to God to help him get over this problem quickly. I was all over the place and so I spoke with Pastor Guy.

Over the past few days, I had been so alone. Jude was not well so we were unable to go and visit, and he had karate training for the next two days. Also, I might have a new partner – I would have to wait and see. I decided to ask him to come to karate tomorrow.

Wesley was doing better. His oxygen came down and I would see him later. When I did he looked better, although his oxygen was up again.

I had so many emotions running through my head. Trevor and I had finally gone our separate ways; it was the end of an era. I was now seeing Albert. Albert seemed to think he was a great catch; time will tell.

Eventually Wesley's oxygen came down and he was doing better. They discovered that he had a streptococcus infection, but the clarithromycin was working.

30 April 2007

Day 246 (60 + 1)

Again, Wesley's oxygen improved – it got down to 29%. Nothing else changed. He was on continuous CPAP, but he looked like he was over the worst. Prayers can be answered, and in Wesley's case, more were answered than not. Still no word from his dad.

May

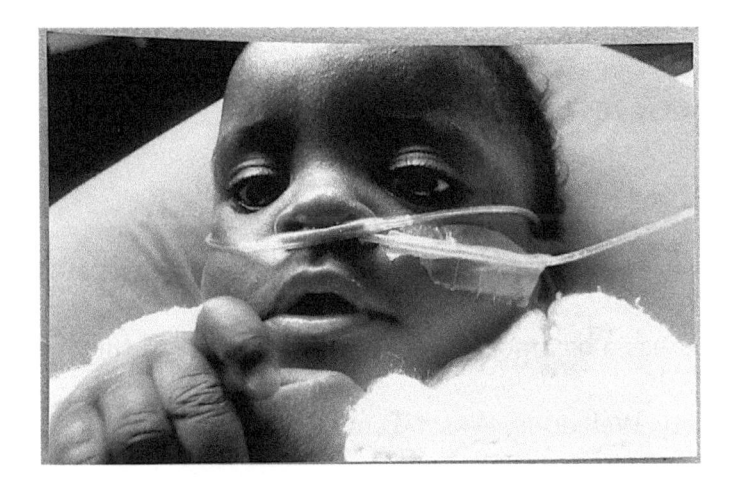

1 May 2007

Day 247 (60 + 2)

Throughout all of this, Wesley had not been weighed. I didn't mind really, but it was one of the only things that I could feel good about, something to hold on to. He was taking one bottle a day. He had amazed everyone with his progress. I prayed for that and it happened. Thank you, Lord. Thank you, Jesus. He also had good gases – well done, my little miracle boy.

He was 11 hours on and 1 hour off CPAP.

2 May 2007

Day 248 (60 + 3)

Wesley tolerated his time off CPAP. I gave him a bath because he was a bit smelly, and I cleaned his ears as they were very dirty. Well done, Wes. I went to see Albert today.

Wesley was weighed today: 5.72 kg, up 70g. He was 10 hours on and 2 hours off CPAP.

3 May 2007

Day 249 (60 + 4)

Again, he tolerated his time off; he had good gases so he could be taken off for longer. He was still on antibiotics for the moment, and his oxygen was between 24% and 29%. Wesley took two bottles while either on CPAP or just oxygen.

He was 9 hours on and 3 hours off twice a day now.

4 May 2007

Day 250 (60 + 5)

Jude was finally given the all-clear and so we were able to visit Wesley as a family. Jude changed his nappy, held him and gave him his bottle while on and off CPAP. Alison was looking after him. Today was a milestone for Wesley, 200 days on the NICU. I will bring a picture of Wesley when he was first born as they were going to produce a certificate saying, '200 days in the NICU'.

He was 8 hours on and 4 hours off twice a day now.

5 May 2007

Day 251 (60 + 6)

Wesley tolerated his time off, so there could be another increase. He looked so good; my emotions were running wild. I looked around the unit and wished I could talk to and comfort all the people with small babies and give them hope and pray for them all, but it is such a personal thing, they needed time to adjust to the world of NICU.

Wesley had good gases, so they would try him for longer tomorrow. He was 7 hours on and 5 hours off twice now. He was weighed today: 5.76 kg, up 40 g.

6 May 2007

Day 252 (61)

Wesley was 6 hours off. He did very well and did not have gas. I gave him a bottle, after which he went right to sleep.

I was feeling a bit anxious about Albert. It might be too soon for a relationship, but I would leave it to God.

Back to work on Tuesday – again I would leave it to God. I had so many emotions about the future, they were all muddled.

7 May 2007

Day 253 (61 + 1)

Wesley was really surprising me with his progress off CPAP,

thank you, God. He did well during the day when he was off, and he had good blood gases, so the same regime would be adopted for tomorrow. Emotionally I felt anxious about the amount of time Wesley was coming off. Thank you, Lord Jesus.

No word from Albert.

He now weighed 5.79 kg, up 30 g. He was 5 hours on and 7 hours off twice a day.

8 May 2007

Day 254 (61 + 2)

Back to work today and emotions were high. I was not feeling well so I could not visit Wesley this morning as I had diarrhoea. Wesley was tolerating his time off; he was being fed every 4 hours and taking some of his bottle. He'd had a good night, took all his bottle and was happy with 7 hours off. He was off for 7 hours again today and really tolerated it.

9 May 2007

Day 255 (61 + 3)

Wesley did not have gas after his time off, and he took all his bottle every 4 hours this morning. There was a change during ward rounds: he did 8 hours off.

Back at work, I felt lost. Wesley was surprising us all. I contacted the hospital and he was doing fine, might even be taken off for longer. All this time at work meant I was not with him. I had to stay away until Thursday.

He was tolerating 4 hours on and 8 hours off twice a day.

10 May 2007

Day 256 (61 + 4)

Wesley was again surprising us. His blood gases were low and so he was coming off for 9 hours twice a day. This evening he was due back at 6 pm, but he was left for 10 hours so I could cuddle him. He had good gases and I put him to sleep. He was due to come off again at 10 pm.

He weighed 5.848 kg (12 lb 14 oz), up 58 g.

11 May 2007

Day 257 (61 + 5)

Wesley did 9 hours last night – he had a good night, good gases. He was doing well.

They decided during the ward rounds to take him off for 10 hours twice a day. I was staying away. I had not kissed my boy since his last episode, and he was so near to coming off that I felt very anxious sometimes because it might get spoiled again.

12 May 2007

Day 258 (61 + 6)

Again, he had a good night: 2 hours on and 10 hours off, and he had good gases. They decided during the ward rounds to leave him off all the time. When they told me that, I felt so blessed. Thank you, God, my saviour and healer.

I also stayed away today as I seemed to have a cold coming on. I visited in the evening and I gave Wesley a bath and he loved it. Would he tolerate being off CPAP?

13 May 2007

Day 259 (62)

I bought Wesley some new clothes. He'd done well overnight. He had been off a long time, nearly 24 hours, and he had good gases. They took another gas at midnight, it was good. What a little fighter, bless him and glory be to the Father.

He now weighed 5.906 kg, up 58 g. He was now permanently off CPAP and on oxygen.

14 May 2007

Day 260 (62 + 1)

Wesley's machine had gone. He was now on a nasal cannula.

I was still in shock, but I trusted in the Lord. Wesley had been transferred to special care and as such was high dependency, but he was off the machine and on a small bit of oxygen. I was happy but scared – this was when I should be at home to spend time with him, but I was back at work.

He now weighed 5.89 kg, down 16 g.

15 May 2007

Day 261 (62 + 2)

Back at work, I phoned the hospital. Wesley was doing well on the cannula, happy and content. I saw him in the afternoon; he looked good, but he was fast asleep. I talked to him. He was in his chair and I did not like the way he was positioned. I laid him down in his bed and fed him, then I went to take Jude to karate.

16 May 2007

Day 262 (62 + 3)

I felt so vulnerable and emotional. I thought I should be with Wesley during the day, but I needed to earn money.

Wesley had a fine day. When I arrived at the hospital he was trying to sleep, so I called him. I took him out for a cuddle and praised God in song while I fed him. He had blood tests and didn't cry so much as moan; he was upset and angry, so he was talking a lot. That gave me mixed emotions – should I laugh or be upset?

17 May 2007

Day 263 (62 + 4)

Wesley had a good night. He had his stoma bag changed. 20% of oxygen, which he had maintained for the past 3 days. Every day I praised God for my little boy and how well he was progressing. It looked like we were going home very soon, and by the grace of God this would happen.

18 May 2007

Day 264 (62 + 5)

I had to talk to the doctors today, Dr April and Dr Able, so I took the day off work. Wesley was doing fine, on 20% of oxygen. He was in his chair and he wanted to jump when he was placed to stand on his legs. He was good, but he did not want to take a bottle. They had to change his bag, so I did not give him a hug. Chris, the going-home nurse, would be coming to visit next week about the oxygen.

19 May 2007

Day 265 (62 + 6)

Mary looked after Wesley today. It was very stressful at one point; I asked her to leave him alone. She was the nurse who had ignored my instructions a while back, which had caused him to be in pain and more distress than he needed to be.

Wesley was doing fine, and that gave me a lot of time to think. It seemed that everything was coming back to me about when Wesley was born; feelings were now coming to the surface.

We visited Wesley early, then I went back in the afternoon. He was doing fine, but he hadn't had any bottles.

20 May 2007

Day 266 (63)

Wesley was doing fine, but now he wouldn't take any of his bottles. *God, what is wrong with him? Please help.* While I was giving Wesley his bottle (he took 40 ml), he opened his mouth and I saw it was very white. I told the nurse that I thought he had thrush, and the doctor agreed and said this was linked to why he wouldn't take his bottle.

21 May 2007

Day 267 (63 + 1)

Work was funny – I fell asleep at the computer. I spoke to the nurse who was going to come to see the house and order the oxygen. I was seeing Wesley every afternoon, with Jude coming to the hospital after school. Wesley was doing fine and was being well looked after. He was seen by a physio, who said he was surprising everyone with his development. I gave him a wash and put on his Babygro before leaving this evening, very tired.

He now weighed 5.944 kg, up 54 g.

22 May 2007

Day 268 (63 + 2)

Wesley was coming home; they were making plans. I could hardly believe it. I didn't feel that I could relax yet – it was still early days and everything was happening in stages. Stage 1: oxygen was ordered from the Oxygen gas supply company, they delivered the oxygen cylinders and the condenser unit; Stage 2: I finished work early and went home to wait for Chris, who would come and assess my home. Albert was also there and we agreed the condenser unit for the oxygen should be in the front room.

I saw Wesley late today at 6 pm and then had to go to pick up Jude. We were getting everything ready. Wesley would be transferred to paediatrics tomorrow morning – we were on our way.

23 May 2007

Day 269 (63 + 3)

I took another annual leave day to facilitate Wesley's move to paediatrics. My manager was not happy; he did not understand why I needed the day off! I suppose I should not have been surprised at his attitude. He was the one who had come to visit with me in the NICU and been broody after seeing all the sick babies on monitors – he was a very strange man.

I felt sad when we went to say goodbye to the staff on the NICU. It was a brand-new day and we took some good pictures, some with the doctors and nurses. We moved to

PICU; Paediatrics was a shock to the system. Wesley was fine. We introduced him to television – he wanted to watch *Countdown*, which might have had something to do with the noise and the buzzer, or maybe the music and the clock. He didn't want CBeebies.

Wesley was looked after by Brenda and Julie for his first night on paediatrics.

24 May 2007

Day 270 (63 + 4)

Wesley had a good night and he was washed this morning by Julie. When I phoned, his oxygen had gone up by 30% and was now at 60%. What was going on? They took bloods and an X-ray of his chest. They just needed time to get to know him.

On another note, the oxygen machine and canisters were being delivered tomorrow. I would work from home – I'm not sure what I did at home, maybe admin.

25 May 2007

Day 271 (63 + 5)

Wesley has been put on a High Energy milk formula, which I'm not sure can be bought in the shops. I saw him this morning and he looked well. His oxygen was down to 30%, which was good. Back at home, the oxygen was delivered at 9:30 am, so I did not have to wait too long.

I went to see Wesley at 2 pm. I was not too bothered about Wesley's bottle, the dietician suggested weaning him onto fruit and veg. I was looking after my baby; I felt like his mum.

26 May 2007

Day 272 (63 + 6)

I was a bit overwhelmed that Wesley was in another new place, paediatrics, with new nurses and a new routine. He was still on 30% of oxygen, doing well. The X-ray showed a shadow, I dismissed that there was anything wrong with him this was his time for coming home. He would be home by the end of the week, by God's grace.

He tasted banana delight and he enjoyed it so much he took 10 spoons. Then milk, tube fed, but he was not overly concerned about that. Wesley had been weighed twice; I needed to update his red book.

He was looked after by Rose and Mandy. He now weighed 6.286 kg, up 342 g.

27 May 2007

Day 273 (64)

Jude stayed at Aunty Sally's house. I went to visit Wesley early as we were travelling to Watford for mass. Wesley took 19 weaning spoons of food, but he did not want the bottle. He had a good day, nothing new to report. He seemed to be taking all his feeds and medicines fine; there did not seem to be as much vomiting. He was looked after by Ronald and Lesley.

28 May 2007

Day 274 (64 + 1)

I had an argument with Wesley's dad; it seemed that he did not want to be part of Wesley's life. For all the time Wesley had been in the hospital, I was lucky if Trevor had visited a total of nine times. But the important thing for me was that Wesley was getting ready to come home.

Wesley had a good night, feeding and changing well, and he slept all through the night. The doctor saw him and was pleased with his progress. He would be given olive oil every evening for cradle cap; it would be rubbed into his scalp as Wesley was always scratching his head. It sounds weird, but I did not know he could do this.

I was feeling very tired as I had returned to work.

Jude stayed at Aunt Sally's house again. Wesley was looked after by Kevin and Ruby.

29 May 2007

Day 275 (64 + 2)

I again went to work early as Jude had the week off. I also had baby massage training in the afternoon – I was really looking forward to it as it was a way to bond with Wesley because we had been apart.

The massage went well; Wesley seemed to enjoy it. It was a bit harder to do because he had the stoma on his stomach. I would be going in to see him early tomorrow as Jude and me were going shopping for him to come home. We needed some sheets and so many different things.

30 May 2007

Day 276 (64 + 3)

I visited the hospital early today as I had promised to spend time with Jude at work. I wanted him to get some pictures of the disused station on the London Underground. This was or is a station that used to be in operation, it is in-between two

Stations. You could only get on it by stopping the train in the tunnel and getting off, only something you could do if you worked there.

We had a good day and Wesley had a very good day. I did not see him for very long, but he'd had a very good night, which was a blessing. He'd started weaning, but he was not interested in sucking a teat. I was not sure what to do, but he was taking pureed food, so that was a plus. I was very tired, but I would see Wesley in the morning – the assessment meeting date.

31 May 2007

Day 277 (64 + 4)

Big meeting today: the decision was made to send Wesley home. After 9 months, he was coming home. Thank you, Lord. Thank you, Jesus. I left the hospital to pick up some more bits for him.

Wesley was coming home for the weekend, but he would still be assigned a nurse and I was to take him back to the hospital if I needed to, and then the official sign-off would be Monday. I couldn't wait, but I would – I had been waiting so long, I didn't want to jinx it. Could I jinx it? It's funny what goes through your head when you have been waiting so long.

June

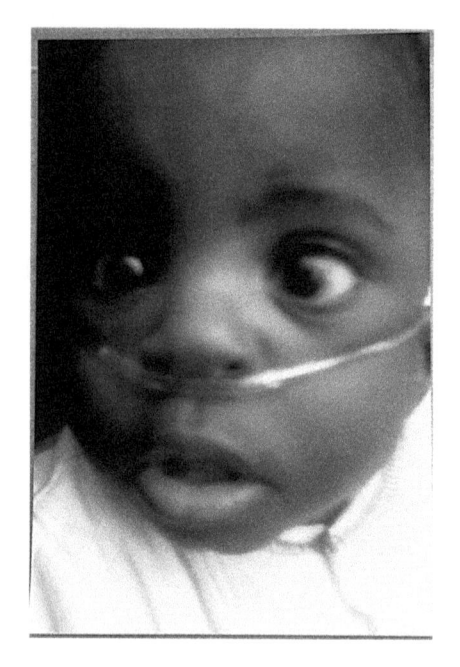

1 June 2007

Day 278 (64 + 5)

Wesley was home. I felt overwhelmed. His cot and everything were set up in my room and Jude would also sleep in my room, all three of us together. I had to run around and pick up syringes and all the feeding kit Wesley would need.

We were home. It felt strange. My boy was home after 9 months, wow! The oxygen was working well; we had a long lead so that I could move around the house. God is a great healer. He is a great God! I held Wesley all through his feed this evening. I sent a message to his dad but got no response.

2 June 2007

Day 279 (64 + 6)

The first morning waking up with my boy at home. Wesley was fine overnight, but it took a while for me to get an aspirate from him. He was being tube fed and I had to check before every feed that the tube had not moved and was still in his stomach, otherwise if it moved, it could be on his lungs. I felt very scared that his milk would not go down the right way. I gave him some solid food, which he seemed to enjoy. It felt good to have both my boys at home. Roy and Mike, Wesley's uncles, visited us at home, and so did Sally and her kids.

3 June 2007

Day 280 (65)

No visitors today, but Albert came round and I took Wesley to meet the neighbours. All day we were free of any visitors; we were able to spend time as a family. I was very busy and did not feel that I had enough time for anything but Wesley. Jude had to organise himself for his trip tomorrow. I kept looking closely at Wesley to make sure he was okay.

4 June 2007

Day 281 (65 + 1)

Jude had gone for the week and Wesley and I would be going back to the hospital to be officially discharged. I did not have time to visit NICU; I would go on Friday. Wesley could now have three meals a day, so I had to plan them. We needed some cereals and baby rice. He was not well, it looked like his nose was very sore – I would check it out tomorrow.

5 June 2007

Day 282 (65 + 2)

Wesley had a good night, although he felt a little cold. I'm not sure why, but when I took his temperature it was always lower than normal, between 35.6 and 36.5, no matter how much I tried to get him warm. I had to keep an eye on his temperature – I did not want him to overheat, but he just seemed cold. It was something else to obsess over.

We went to the doctors with my prescription, and I also bought some food for Wesley; he liked certain baby foods. We went out for our first walk.

Wesley had a good night, but in the early hours of the morning he wanted to play. It was the best feeling – I was not tired, just unbelievably happy.

6 June 2007

Day 283 (65 + 3)

Very tired today. I did not get any syringes in the post and realised this was because *no one knew that Wesley had been discharged*. I had a discussion with the community nurses, who referred me to outpatients. No one knew he had gone home – how could that be? He was in the hospital for 9 months – did they think he was never coming home? The dietician called; she did not know that we had gone home, but she ordered all that we needed. I concentrated on the things I could control, like the oxygen order.

We had a meeting at the hospital. I was there and all the departments were there. We agreed that he was now discharged – how could they not have known that meant he was *going home?* Wesley was doing fine, thank God, but I felt so overwhelmed!

I had to pick up Wesley's meds; it was two carrier bags full. He had things from Gaviscon for his reflux to vitamins for his well-being. I wasn't sure about his meds list and why there was so much of it. I do know that he went onto a special milk that was full of calories.

Jude was away and it was time for me to bond with Wesley, but it was so much to take on by myself. I missed Jude and wanted him home with us.

7 June 2007

Day 284 (65 + 4)

Mum and Aunty Afa were coming today; they were excited. They were not bringing Granny Edin with them, and I felt that was strange, because she was the matriarch of the family and she wanted to see Wesley but could not come to the hospital because she had arthritis in her back, and they stopped all visitors when she was more able.

So was the delivery of all the feeding bottles and the machine for the milk and the syringes – lots of syringes. I would also have to pick up the sodium chloride from the hospital.

Wesley was doing fine. He was a bit sniffly, but that did not worry me. The health visitor came and we had a long chat; I told her how I was feeling. It was overwhelming and I was playing catch-up because people were not doing what they were supposed to. Little did I know that this was something that would follow me round now Wesley was home.

Jude was still at Haven, holiday place in Camber Sands. Mum and Aunty Afa bounced Wesley on their knee. It is a family tradition we must make a baby climb the coconut tree while we sing. They must also hear the lullaby 'Doe doe poor pity'. He was tired from all the jumping, but he was home and engaged.

8 June 2007

Day 285 (65 + 5)

Jude was back today, yippee! We did not go back to the hospital and I was sure Jude was excited. Wesley was doing fine.

My boss felt that I had let him down; he said he had bent over backward to help me. I will explain I worked and then I had a panic attack, so the doctor signed me off work. Wesley had come home and there was no way I was taking him back to the hospital. I had problems with Trevor, the NHS and work – I felt like I was being pushed over the edge. It was intense. Which one should I deal with first? But I came back from this and focused on Wesley, thank you, Lord.

Physio went well and I was advised to buy Wesley a Bembo chair and just keep up with the stimulation to get him to sit up and move around.

9 June 2007

Day 286 (65 + 6)

I tried to have a bit of a lie-in but no such luck. Was I already moaning about having to care for my son? I had been asking for this for months and now I was moaning.

I got up early and talked and played with Wesley. I didn't seem to be taking care of myself. I was feeling anxious all the time and I wasn't sure what was going on with me. I decided to go out, just to Asda.

I had a good day with Jude and Wesley; it was so good having both my children at home. There was no time to cook so we had McDonalds takeout, or was it Chinese? I'm not sure. I was becoming very indecisive; I didn't really have a plan. My past few months had been so planned and rigid, but now they were unorganised and dishevelled.

10 June 2007

Day 287 (66)

Wesley's pre-op was cancelled as there was an outbreak of diarrhoea and vomiting at the hospital, Ward C3, where we would be going. Yes, we were back on the stoma reversal, but again the time was not right. I was not going to think about it – all in God's time. Another date would be arranged. I was quite relieved as I had nothing prepared and I just wanted to stay home. Wesley was fine with it – everything in God's time.

11 June 2007

Day 288 (66 + 1)

I went out for a nice walk with Wes. There's nothing more to say about it, we just spent the day together, taking time out.

12 June 2007

Day 289 (66 + 2)

We had a visit from community nurse, Nikki. She came to check Wesley's sats and to weigh him. Wesley was asleep the whole time, so she left; it would happen on Thursday instead. I was not going to wake my little man; he needed his sleep.

I took Wesley to the doctor's as I thought he might be getting a cold, but everything was fine. I didn't know how to explain my feelings. I did not have a new-born – he was 9 months old or thereabouts – but I felt like I did and I was anxious about every little thing. I was beginning to realise how supported I had been when Wesley was in the hospital and there were so many people to speak with. Now my son was home, but he needed feeding with a tube which could drown him if I didn't set it up right, and when he did a poo I had to scoop it out of the stoma bag and put it in the toilet or his nappy. But God was watching over us.

I had to give Wesley more solids; he needed to bulk up and his organs needed to grow and heal.

13 June 2007

Day 290 (66 + 3)

Jude was at home. We had a good day; we did not have any visitors, which was nice. We travelled to London to see my Granny Edin. It was the first time she had seen Wesley and she cried. His Aunty Carryl was there too and she said his head was misshapen. He was feeding when I took him, but there were too many people and he was sick. I wondered if he felt sick as well.

I had another reason to travel to London: I had to see the board's doctor for work, and she said she would talk to my manager about leaving me alone for about 4 weeks – everything in God's time.

Wesley had cereal, fruit and milk for breakfast; a savoury meal a pudding and milk for lunch; A savoury meal a pudding and milk for dinner; and a rusk with milk for supper.

14 June 2007

Day 291 (66 + 4)

Today I was at home with Wesley, and Jude was also at home. We had a visit from Nikki, the nurse. She did Wesley's saturations (sats) and weighed him; he had put on 200 g or thereabouts, and his sats were good, which meant we were closer to coming off oxygen. Nikki said that at some point she would lower the oxygen with a view to taking him off for an hour, but that would happen the next time she came to visit, not today.

The SALT nurse also came to see Wesley. She had a look at him and we talked about weaning him into taking his milk from a Doydy cup, which has one side higher than the other so that the milk can just pour into his mouth. I was pleased with this outcome, but how was I going manage it if we went out? It was a lot of work. Also, if I fed him too fast, he could choke.

Wesley had had a bad case of thrush while he was in the hospital and after that he did not suck any more. The SALT lady did not know anything. I suppose I was trying to say that I asked if there was a bottle alternative to giving him the Doydy cup as this would be upsetting when we were out. They did not have an alternative, but I remembered the sippy cup with a valve that I used to give Jude so went looking and found it. Wesley had a bad case of thrush and would no longer suck. I researched it myself and found a sip cup by

Avent – if you removed the valve, it would just pour into his mouth, so he took a bottle and would be able to come off the tube feeding very soon. God bless everyone.

15 June 2007

Day 292 (66 + 5)

I gave Wesley a bath; they always had to be well timed because he still had the stoma and if I didn't time it well, he could poo all over me, which was not pleasant! I changed his bag. He was very sore – not the stoma itself, that looked healthy, but the skin where the diadem stuck to hold the stoma in place. I would change him more often.

Jude was at home. Wesley had a blood test in the morning – he did well – and then we went to baby massage class near town. I really enjoyed this bonding session. Wesley really enjoyed being massaged, so I decided to go again next week. It was so much fun; I loved massaging him! Wesley was doing really well and we were trying to get a routine going with his feeds. It would take time. Jesus loves us.

16 June 2007

Day 293 (66 + 6)

It was raining today, so I decided to stay in Luton. We went shopping but I did not have any money to pay because I left my cards at home. I came home and did not really have any dinner. Wesley and Jude were both fine. Wesley was loving his solid food; he was taking solids well and I had also bought him some veg.

17 June 2007

Day 294 (67)

I woke up and decided to take Wesley out for a walk today. It had taken time to settle into a routine of going out, mainly because we'd had no routine apart from the daily trips to the hospital for the past 9 months.

The house was a mess. I had scrubbed and cleaned and bleached and disinfected it just before Wesley came home, but he had only been home for a few days, so I was sure the sanitation hadn't run out yet. The house could wait; I didn't care.

We went for a long walk. It was very nice to be out and about and not on the hospital grounds. We visited a couple of friends. The weather was nice, so we went outside in the garden because it was warm. Then we came home. Feeding Wesley was getting harder; I was trying not to feed him with a tube as he was being weaned and this made things more difficult, but I was changing up the textures and making sure he would eat anything. *Thank you for today, Lord.*

18 June 2007

Day 295 (67 + 1)

I woke up early today, but I did not give Wesley his 6 am feed – I gave him breakfast instead. I was trying to wean him off the milk feed as we were still using the tube and I wanted him on the bottle. Jude stayed home from school again; he was getting to know and bonding with Wesley.

The community nurse visited. Wesley was doing well, no change, which was especially good since we were going to Addenbrooke's. We didn't want to lower his oxygen if it meant he would struggle, which could lead to an infection, which could then lead to higher oxygen and missing his operation again.

We needed to get a regime going for Wesley's solids and his milk, so I would try. Breakfast was a cup of milk, lunch was pudding, and supper was pudding and then a rusk and milk.

19 June 2007

Day 296 (67 + 2)

We went to Addenbrooke's for Wesley's pre-op assessment. The day was here; it had been a long time coming and I was feeling very nervous. I still fed him at 3:30 am because he seemed like he was asking for it, so I gave in. It was probably not the best thing to do, but I wanted him to get a taste for all foods, I just wanted him to eat. We needed him to put on weight, so I would go with it for now.

At Addenbrooke's I changed Wesley two times because he made himself sick. We were at another hospital and they were using all the syringes and different new things on him, and he pulled out his Nasogastric (NG) Intubation tube, his feeding tube. That meant a new tube and an X-ray to check where it was placed in his body. It went well. *Here we go again. Lord, guide and protect us on our short visit.*

20 June 2007

Day 297 (67 + 3)

Wesley woke up after 4 hours for his food – what a smart boy. He had a good night, no desaturations. We were in the hospital regime again and it took a bit of getting used to. The doctor made up a new prescription, and today we would find out if he was having the op.

I saw Dr Ink about Wesley's lungs, then the anaesthetist – they felt that we needed to wait till October/November to perform the op, so we were discharged from Addenbrooke's.

Wesley's lungs had always been an issue. He was on oxygen, and the last time we visited they felt that if he was still on oxygen for the operation, he might end up on life support. They took several X-rays of his lungs and the lung specialist showed me why they wouldn't be doing the operation: his lungs were really wet. They gave him even more medication, this time really targeting his lungs. They also felt that he would have the best chance of getting better and coming off the oxygen now because it was warm, otherwise he might be in hospital for the whole summer.

21 June 2007

Day 298 (67 + 4)

I slept in my own bed tonight. It was great to be home! I agreed with the anaesthetist, Liam: I wanted Wesley home for the summer. There was no rush for the op, so I would wait until God decided.

I had not heard from Albert, but this book is not about him. Trevor seemed to be coming around more! But this book is not about him either.

22 June 2007

Day 299 (67 + 5)

Wesley had a good night. I picked up his medication. I had been feeling very tired. I sometimes found that writing in my diary was a bit boring, or I felt like I didn't have much to say.

On the one hand I was disappointed about the operation because I wanted my son to be put back together, but on the other hand I was blessed to have him home. I had prayed for that and he was happy, always smiling.

Wesley's dad visited this afternoon. *Thank you, Lord, for making him show an interest in Wesley, thank you.*

23 June 2007

Day 300 (67 + 6)

We stopped Wesley's ranitidine today; this was for the reflux from his stomach. It was a very busy Saturday: I went into town with Wesley and Jude because Jude wanted some new trainers.

Wesley was doing well. He was enjoying being home and doing different things. I felt like I did not have enough time in the day; I thought I just needed to get a bit more organised and Wesley needed to be more stimulated. *Lord, I ask for your help and guidance.*

24 June 2007

Day 301 (68)

I woke up early. Guess what? The plug points had gone in the kitchen, so now I had to do something about it. I fixed them, but I was beginning to realise that I had a lot of work to do in the house. It needed vacuuming (again).

Wesley ate very well today; I was very proud of him. He slept through the night till 5 am. *Lord, guide and protect my family.*

25 June 2007

Day 302 (68 + 1)

A very mixed day with Wesley. I had a short fuse and Wesley kept putting his hand very deep in his mouth and getting sick. How could I stop him? He was teething, so he seemed a bit restless. He ate okay today; we would persevere. He woke up for a feed at 4 am. Thank you, Lord.

26 June 2007

Day 303 (68 + 2)

I spoke to the NICU and was advised the operation wouldn't be till October. I had an appointment at the doctors, so I took Wesley. I wanted to go out for a walk afterwards, but the weather looked a bit suspect, so we didn't. We also needed to go to karate when Jude came home.

    Wesley made himself sick for most of the day – it was very stressful and he seemed unwell.

27 June 2007

Day 304 (68 + 3)

Wesley cut his first tooth; he seemed to be in a lot of pain. He would not take his afternoon feed. No solids, but his sats were ok. He had not put on weight; in fact, he had lost 80 g, poor thing. I had to give him Calpol for the pain and some cold toys to soothe his gums. He would just have milk for the next couple of days.

28 June 2007

Day 305 (68 + 4)

Milk feed at 3 am, and then I had to go to Tesco at 4 am. I left Wesley with his brother. I was not gone for too long, but I needed to visit the supermarket.

29 June–7 July 2007

Days 306–314 (68 + 5–13)

We had a mixed few days with Wesley. He was doing fine and feeding, but he was not putting on any weight. We went for the assessment, but he would not have the operation until October/November. He was doing so much now – he was sitting up for 2 minutes at a time and putting things in his mouth.

End

My son was home, finally, after 9 intense months – months that had me living and running on empty. I'm not quite sure how I survived. I don't even remember waking up and putting one foot in front of the other. I'm not sure how I got through this testing time, but I knew I had to!

Epilogue

Wesley finally went to Addenbrooke's Hospital in Cambridge to have his gastric stoma reversed. He had had the original operation when he was just 2 weeks old and weighed about 600 kg, the same as a bag of sugar. They had brought out his bowel and he'd had a stoma for several months.

Now that we were at Addenbrooke's, there were so many things that needed to be done before the operation. Wesley had to have a procedure where they washed out his bowel from the anus; he had to have only clear juices, then water, until his stool was very runny. This went on for several days. They then said that we had to cancel, go home and come back in a few days. I put Wesley back on full feeds, which he was happy about, but the clearing of the bowel from the anus was very painful and even more so for me to have to watch. He cried a lot, and I was not looking forward to watching him have this done again.

We went back in a few days and we followed the same procedure, but they did not do the anal clear. They said it should not be done, it was painful and he had not used his bowel for months, so it was not needed. I was glad they didn't do it, but angry that he'd had to go through so much pain when it was not necessary.

The lung specialist, the gastroenterologist and the anaesthetist came to see me before the surgery. The lung specialist came because Wesley was still on oxygen; he took an X-ray of his lungs, which were cloudy, which meant Wesley would probably end up on full ventilation during and after the operation. I was worried but refused to take it on board. I would hold on to God and my belief that he had brought my son through the worst and we were reaching the finish line.

Wesley went down to surgery at around 9:30 am and I was told the operation would take no more than an hour and a half, as it was straightforward; they were most worried about Wesley going onto life support. After 3 hours there was no sign of them, so I asked the nurses on the ward if they could find out what was happening. It turned out they were still in surgery and Wesley was still on oxygen. When the surgeons did the original operation, they did not clear his bowel, they just brought part of it out and left the rest inside. When they checked his bowel this time it was full of infection that had lain dormant and had to be cut out, hence why this operation was taking so long.

He was finally brought up to the ward after nearly 6 hours and he was not even on oxygen. He was taken to PICU and a consultant and nurse were left with him. I was told about the operation – it had gone well, but there was a lot of cutting and stitching that had left him with many lesions on his bowel. They were hopeful that the operation had been a success, but we would be on the ward for 5 days at least until his bowel started to work. They also said Wesley was in the honeymoon period again, and they expected him to desaturate very quickly within the next hour. Again, I dismissed this in Jesus' name and believed that my son would not need much oxygen.

An hour went by and he still did not need oxygen; they said it would happen very soon. Two hours passed, then three, and the lung specialist said, "I am a top specialist and I cannot explain what has happened here. We are going to move Wesley onto the general ward – we cannot see anything else happening, he just needs time for everything to begin working. We need his bowel to begin working."

I said, "I do not doubt your ability, but I have said from the start that there is a higher power at work in my son's life and some things that have happened throughout his care cannot be explained."

We spent a few days on the ward. Everything went like clockwork and Wesley was on about 10% oxygen, but only because he had just had surgery; he would come off it soon. Wesley had always been a smiling child ever since he had come home, and one thing we noticed was he had no smile.

We took one last picture with the nurses before we made our way home.

When we got home and Wesley saw his brother, he had the biggest smile for him – I guess he had not lost his smile, but he held it for his brother. Although I know there are many other obstacles to climb, I am so thankful to the many people who helped us along the way, the many friends I made and the many churches that prayed for us. It is humbling to know that, although we don't know them, there are churches out there who know about the miracle that is my son, who spent 9 months on the outside and came home.

Thank you, God, for giving me the

strength to

write my truth.